Reviews of Take a M...

This book is a goldmine of useful and fast ...   ...f ourselves in those stress-laden and challenging moments that must of us encounter in our everyday lives. Packed with different tips to pick ourselves up when we are down, or exhausted, experiencing low moods, have no energy, are angry or frustrated.

~ Nick The Nosey Genealogist

The tone is gentle but encouraging; there is no bossing or cajoling - just a simple recognition that life can be full of problems and stumbling blocks but that they can be tackled successfully step by step. We are all unique and the book emphasises methods by which we can each become 'our best self' and live out the life we are meant to have.

~ Nicky Winter

Thorough and insightful, the book explains physiological and psychological measures in a simple, bite size style which is both easy to follow and straightforward to apply in everyday life. In addition, the book demystifies meditation making it uncomplicated and doable for those who might have considered it daunting. I recommend this book as a comprehensive and practical guide to better equip you to deal with life's problems and challenges.

~ Brandon

I have no hesitation in recommending this book to everyone, especially if you have a tendency to put other people's needs before your own.

~ Christine K

I have been going through this little gem of a book and it's brilliant.

~ *old1*

I've re-read Jo's book a number of times now since buying and each time I pick out more little hints that seem so simple but are so effective in helping me refocus and relax. As a senior citizen, I find sleep does not come easily to me especially at the right time and by following her advice, I am both getting off to sleep quicker and easier as well as sleeping longer.

~ *MadHusband*

This is a wonderful book. It is a small investment that will help you for years to come.

~ *Clifford Martin*

TAKE A MOMENT

33 Fast Fixes to Relax, Restore and Refocus Your Mind and Body in 10 Minutes or Less

JO FRENCH

Copyright © 2024 by Jo French

First Printing: 2024

Version 1.2

All rights reserved

In a Nutshell Books

This book or any of its parts may not be reproduced or used in any manner whatsoever without the express written permission of the author and publisher. However, brief quotations in a book review or scholarly journal are permitted.

Authors and their publications mentioned in this work and bibliography have their copyright protection. All brand and product names used in this book are trademarks, registered trademarks, or trade names and belong to the respective owners.

The author is unassociated with any product or vendor in this book.

ISBN 9798860508361

To my friends, family and all the healthcare professionals who have helped me to learn what is important and what makes a good, happy and peaceful life – thank you for everything.

Contents

Part 1 – About This Book 19
    Why I Wrote This Book.. 19
    Why You Need This Book 21
    How to Use This Book 23
    Some Words of Comfort... 26

Part 2 – 33 Fast Fixes to Relax, Restore and Refocus 31
    Fast Fixes for When You Wake 31
    #1 – When you just don't want to do anything 32
    #2 – When you can't get going 35
    #3 – When you need a lift 36
    #4 – When you feel sad 39
    Fast Fixes for Mornings 41
    #5 – When pressure at work makes you feel stressed 41
    #6 – When you feel overwhelmed 43
    #7 – When you feel anger rising 45
    #8 – When you are lacking motivation 46
    Fast Fixes for Lunchtimes 49
    #9 – When you feel you need to escape for a while 49
    #10 – When you need to make time for yourself 51
    #11 – When you wonder why you should bother 54
    #12 – When the day seems too long already 56
    #13 – When you feel closed in 58
    Fast Fixes for Afternoons 61
    #14 – When you are finding it hard to keep going 61
    #15 – When you need to concentrate and focus 64
    #16 – When you feel wired 66
    #17 – When you feel anxious or stressed 68
    #18 – When you feel tired and achy 71
    Fast Fixes for Evenings 75
    #19 – When you can't unwind 75
    #20 – When your mind is going around and around 78

#21 – When life feels hard going 80
Fast Fixes for Bedtime 85
#22 – When you feel lost 85
#23 – When you feel depressed 87
#24 – When you are unsettled and can't sleep 89
Fast Fixes for Anytime 93
#25 – When you need to calm down 93
#26 – When you feel down 95
#27 – When you need to change your mood 97
#28 – When you need comfort and reassurance 99
#29 – When you feel lonely 102
#30 – When you feel over tired 103
#31 – When life seems boring and pointless 106
#32 – When you are feeling negative 108
#33 – When you are losing hope 111

Part 3 – Your 30-Day Challenge 115
Week 1 – Days 1 to 7 116
Week 2 – Days 8 to 14 117
Week 3 – Days 15 to 21 119
Week 4 – Days 22 to 28 120
Week 5 – Days 29 and 30 121
Tracking Your Progress 122
What Next? 123

Part 4 – Conclusion 129

Glossary of Terms 133

References 143

Resources and Further Reading 147

One Last Thing… 151

Fast Fix Finder 153

Index 155

Acknowledgements

I would love to acknowledge the amazing people who helped me to create and finish this book.

My husband Mike for being a valuable sounding board and for his help with the images and cover.

My Mum June for always being there and supporting me whatever I do.

Breeda McBrearty and many other healthcare professionals who helped me in my own health journey.

Chris Payne for his invaluable support and advice in the creative and technical aspects of writing books. I would not have written this book without his guidance and encouragement.

The other members of Chris' writing group, who inspired and motivated me with their own book writing and publishing journeys and successes.

Rob Cornish for introducing me to Chris, for which I will be forever grateful.

Farah Canicosa for her kind assistance with the initial cover design and with technical queries.

And finally, I thank you, the reader, for taking a chance on this book. I genuinely hope you gain something truly great from embracing the ideas I share with you. If it changes your life, I would love to hear from you!

Jo x   jo@inanutshellbooks.com

About the Author

Dr Jo French has an innate curiosity about everything. She could never decide which direction to take as she is fascinated by many diverse things, so she has degrees in both arts/humanities: a first-class honours degree in *Humanities* and a PhD in the  *Philosophy of Mind and Consciousness*; and sciences: an MSc in *Compuer Science*.

She has lectured at university in philosophy, computer science and cognitive science, was a university academic and wellbeing mentor, an equestrian coach and ran a very successful £1m+ internet business.

One thing she always wanted to be, consistently throughout all those years, was a writer. She trained with the London School of Journalism and wrote fiction and non-fiction, having a number of books, features and short stories published.

She has a particular interest in women's health and the health challenges of modern life.

Jo lives in the beautiful Cotswolds in the UK, which inspires her to work hard so she never has to leave. She writes because she can't not write and because her passion is to help people to live calmer, more peaceful and happier lives.

> *Peace of mind is your richest treasure. See that you do nothing which may rob you of your peace of mind. Regulate your life in such a way that it adds to your inner calm and does not take away your peace.*
>
> **His Holiness the Dalai Lama**

Part 1
About This Book

Part 1 – About This Book

Why I Wrote This Book

As an academic, workaholic, high-achieving perfectionist, it wasn't surprising that, in my 30s, I suffered from major burnout, simply from working too hard and not taking proper care of myself.

The effect it had on my life was catastrophic. I lost quite a few years of which, looking back, I now have very little memory. And those were years that were unproductive too, which was very unsatisfying.

It is a surprisingly common experience, especially for women who try to juggle everything – work, home and family life. They often experience the strange effect of losing their memories of this time, so much so that it even has a name – *The Amnesia Years*. I am sure the same happens to men too.

In an effort to heal myself from a very dark place, I became very interested in health. I wasn't going to fundamentally change my personality, so I knew I needed to find a way to take better care of myself and fully recover. I was also sure that I didn't want to suffer from the same thing again.

I needed to work out how I could still work hard, achieve a

lot and yet take care of myself at the same time.

I spent a lot of time reading, researching and trying things out. I went down a lot of blind alleys with things that simply didn't work, although I also noted things that may not have worked for me but that I knew had worked for other people.

All this took me a long time. I often wished there had been a book that just told me, simply and succinctly, what to do to make myself feel better in those darker moments. What a difference it would have made to have had something like that close by that I could just reach out for when I felt I needed some help and support.

Within these pages, I hope I have created the book I always wished I'd had. It is my gift to you, in the hope it will provide a comforting friend who will always be there for you and who will always have something to say that will help to lift your mood, get you going, calm you down or just hold your hand and give you back your faith and belief in life and in yourself.

Wherever you are and whatever is happening for you, take a moment for yourself, take a deep breath and try some of these techniques. I truly hope you find calm, peace, focus and direction in your day.

Part 1 – About This Book

Why You Need This Book

It is not easy to live calmly and peacefully in the hectic pace of a demanding 21st century life. But you can, and *must*, take time for yourself.

The tips in this book are designed for busy people who have hectic lives, but who need to learn to take a very short time out for themselves, especially when your day is challenging. We all need to be sure that our health and wellbeing remain a priority in our lives, whatever is going on for us. I know, to my own cost, the effects of not doing that.

Time taken to take care of yourself is not selfish or self-indulgent, it is essential. Even just 5 minutes a day will make a huge difference. It's really important.

There is nothing you need to take more care of than your own inner sense of calm and wellbeing. Do not neglect it and do not let anyone compromise it for you.

If you can take 2, 3 or 5 minutes out of your day two or three times a day, you will feel the benefit immediately and it will build over time.

> *Self-care means giving yourself permission to pause.*
> **Cecilia Tran**

Here are my best discoveries to date – a compilation of hints, tips and techniques that I learned to help myself and I share them here with you.

I hope you will find something useful in these pages. Please feel free to dip in and out as much as you wish. Use the ones that help you and don't bother with the ones that don't. You know yourself and what works for you.

Most of all, take care of yourself. You are unique, special and important in this world and there are people who need and love you. You owe it to yourself to be the best possible version of you for yourself and for them.

Part 1 – About This Book

How to Use This Book

This book provides you with 33 different *Fast Fixes* to pick yourself up when you're feeling down. This could be when you're suffering from low mood, lack of energy or motivation, when you are angry, frustrated, tired or stressed, when you need some way to kickstart your day or when you just need to take a breath and take a break.

Anytime you need a little help in your day, you can dip in and out and choose something to try.

The 33 *Fast Fixes* are designed to be short, quick to read and easy to do, wherever you are. Each one is described in detail to give you a clear view of what is involved, so that you can quickly choose which ones work for you and what is right at that particular moment.

This book is meant for you to pick up and dip into when you are feeling down. If you find something that works for you amongst its pages, then mark the pages where you found *Fast Fixes* that were particularly helpful to make it easier to find them again when you want to go back to them. You can also search for them in the Fast Fix Finder at the back of this book or in the index.

TAKE A MOMENT

There are all kinds of different ideas here, so you should find some that will work for you.

Some of them may introduce you to new techniques you have not encountered before, such as Emotional Freedom Technique (EFT) or Mindfulness Meditation. If any of those work for you, I warmly encourage you to explore the techniques further beyond the scope of this book. To help you with this, I have added some resources and further reading at the back of the book, plus a Glossary of Terms to check terminology.

I hope this book gives you a lift when you need it. It is just here to be a friend, to hold your hand in those difficult moments that we all have when we need a little bit of extra help.

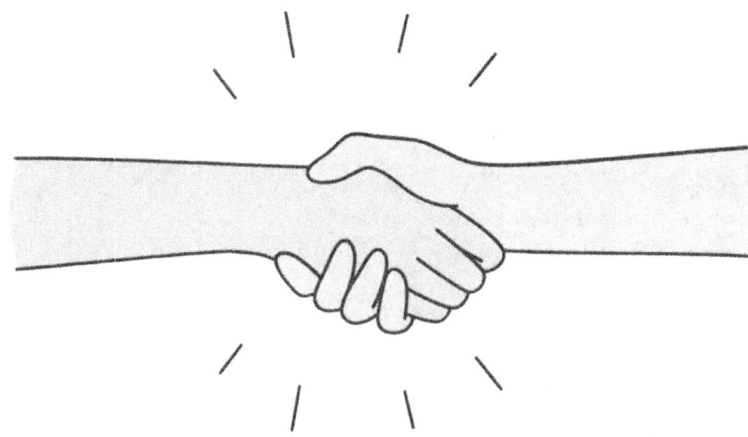

Part 1 – About This Book

One thing I believe is that we are all here to help each other. If you have any extra ideas, not contained in this book, that you have found help to give you a lift in moments like these, please feel free to send them to me so that I can include them in the next book, with a thank you to you on the relevant page. Maybe you will be able to help someone else.

In the meantime, I send you my warmest wishes for a happy, healthy and peaceful life.

TAKE A MOMENT

Some Words of Comfort

The tips and techniques in this book are designed to be complimentary. They are not intended to be a replacement for proper medical advice. If you are suffering from depression, anxiety or any other mood issue that does not resolve itself within 2 to 3 weeks, please seek medical advice from your GP or therapist.

Part 1 – About This Book

You can also try to reach out to a friend, family member or work colleague. Remember, there is always someone out there who will be willing to listen and people who will be able to help.

Although it is sometimes easy to think that no one has ever felt the way you do right now, please be assured this is not the case. You may be surprised to find how many people will put an arm around you and say they have felt the same way themselves. There are lots of people who will understand.

We all have times when we are not coping so well and sometimes there may be no obvious external reason for it. This is completely normal and you are not alone. Please seek help as soon as you can. Never give up. There are always ways forward and better times ahead.

Part 2
33 Fast Fixes to Relax, Restore and Refocus

Part 2

Part 2 – 33 Fast Fixes to Relax, Restore and Refocus

Fast Fixes for When You Wake

First thing in the morning can be a challenging time for many people.

While some lucky, early-morning types can jump out of bed feeling refreshed and happy and ready for the day, the less fortunate can struggle to find motivation to get up and can feel low at first. This is due to a drop in the levels of hormones and neurotransmitters, like serotonin and dopamine, overnight which can cause low mood. A drop in blood sugar, due to the overnight fast, can also cause a lack of energy.

Here are some *Fast Fixes* that can be easy and fast pick-me-ups for first thing in the morning.

#1 – When you just don't want to do anything

Get Moving First and Feel Better

We all have days when we just don't feel like doing anything.

Sometimes it is just hard to get started. You feel lethargic and unmotivated. You promise yourself you will get going in a minute, when you feel better. But you don't.

I have read and listened to hundreds of self-help books over the years and one of the most useful tips I ever heard, which I wished I had learned many years earlier, is that you will never feel better just sitting there.

The simple message is: don't wait until you feel better, just get moving and *then* you will feel better.

MOVE → 2 → IMPROVE

This really effective 2-step technique can be used anywhere and at any time. It is a particularly useful way to motivate yourself when you feel no incentive to get out of bed in the morning.

It is too easy to sit in the dark or lie on the bed feeling sorry for yourself, promising yourself that when you start to feel better, then you'll get up and get on with something.

But, sadly, this doesn't work. All that happens is that you're going to sit or lie there forever. You can stay there for the rest of your life, but it won't help.

Part 2 – 33 Fast Fixes to Relax, Restore and Refocus

If you want to feel better when you're moping or feeling sad or depressed, you need to make yourself get up and start moving before you will feel better, not the other way around.

Your lack of energy and motivation is caused by a drop in your adrenaline levels. It is purely a chemical imbalance that's causing you to lie there moping and feeling bad. It doesn't mean anything. But as long as you continue to stay where you are, your chemicals will stay at depressed levels. The only way to stimulate your adrenaline levels to increase is to actually get up and start moving.

It's a question of mind over matter. You just need to decide to make the effort to get up, however hard it is.

> *We generate fears while we sit. We overcome them by action.*
> **Henry Link**

Drag yourself up, using your arms to hoist yourself up if necessary (or a helping hand, if there is a friend nearby), and do something, however small. Take a walk around the garden, walk down to the local shop or just get up and make yourself a cup of tea. Any activity that you can convince yourself to try will make your adrenaline levels increase and you will feel better almost instantly.

It doesn't take very long at all.

As soon as you get up, you start getting your systems going again and then you'll find you can do a little bit more and then a bit more. Before you know it, you're up and running and feeling hugely better.

TAKE A MOMENT

Next time you're lying there moping and convincing yourself that you'll get up as soon as you feel better, remember that you could be there forever, waiting for things to improve, wasting the day and wasting your life.

It's a bit like turning the ignition on a car engine to get the first spark. It takes a bit of effort from the spark plugs. But once the engine is running, you're off. Try it. You'll be amazed. And you'll soon be getting on with your day.

Part 2 – 33 Fast Fixes to Relax, Restore and Refocus

#2 – When you can't get going

Touch Your Toes

This may seem like a strange one to start your day, but it really does work.

Touching your toes is a great stretcher for your lower back. Not only does this help with your flexibility and the strength of your core muscles, plus it works your hamstrings and calves, but it also allows blood to drain to your head, which can often be helpful when you need a first-thing-in-the-morning pick-me-up.

Scientists have long understood that there is a direct correlation between brain activity and blood flow. More blood to your head means more glucose and oxygen for your brain, which enhances the brain's capacity for clear thinking.

The brain is a very hungry organ. It has no storage facility so it needs both oxygen and glucose to be readily available at all times.

The recommended glucose requirement of an adult is 200g and the brain uses 130g of this every day.

Likewise, the brain has huge oxygen requirements. The brain comprises only 2% of our body but it requires 20-25% of our oxygen intake.

Getting blood to your head will wake you up. You should make sure you take care of your brain by giving it a blood boost and touching your toes can be a great way to do this.

There are other reasons why touching your toes is great for your health. A Japanese study showed that the easier you find touching your toes, the lower your blood pressure will be. It also reduces your risk of heart disease.

If you practice touching your toes, you will find, over a period of time, you will get better and better at it so that you can reach further down. You should aim to try to get your hands flat on the floor in front of your feet or to either side or even cross your hands behind your ankles. Don't worry if you cannot achieve these goals, whatever you can manage will help. Just see how far down you can stretch and then try to go a fraction further. It takes time, but you only need to practice for a couple of minutes a day and it will make a huge difference.

#3 – When you need a lift

Early Morning Light for Wellbeing

Why is early morning sunlight so special and why does it lift your mood?

If you're not a morning person or if you find it hard to sleep at night, getting more exposure to early morning light may be just what you need.

Studies have shown that getting more direct morning light helps to reset your circadian rhythms, our internal 24-hour cycle, which we often refer to as our body clock, making it easier for you to stay alert during the day and get to sleep at night. This is because light is an important signal for your body to know when it is time to wake up and when it is time to go to bed.

Try to get into the habit of going outside first thing in the morning, before you do anything else in your day. Take yourself outside for a short walk, or even just to sit in the garden or some outdoor space where you can let the light filter into your eyes.

Exposure to morning light can also help to increase serotonin, the feel-good chemical in your brain that helps you to stay calm, positive and focused. This can be a great help if you suffer from depression or anxiety.

Another really amazing benefit of early morning sunlight is that it burns fat. Scientists believe that 20 to 30 minutes of morning light between 8am and 12 noon can help to shrink fat cells below the surface of the skin. The earlier in the morning you get it, the more effect it has.

> Every sunrise gives you a new beginning and a new ending. Let this morning be a new beginning to a better relationship and a new ending to the bad memories.
> It's an opportunity to enjoy life, breathe freely, think and love. Be grateful for this beautiful day.
>
> **Norton Juster**

If you find it difficult to get your daily exposure, you can use a daylight lamp or light box. These are especially helpful for people who suffer from Seasonal Affective Disorder (SAD), but they can help anyone by replicating the effects of natural daylight, especially in the winter months when the evenings are darker and the days are shorter.

It is also worth noting that exposure to bright light in the two hours before you go to bed can affect how easily you fall sleep. Bright light reduces your levels of melatonin, the hormone that helps you fall asleep, so it makes sense to reduce your exposure to light later in the day. If you regulate your light exposure so you get more in the morning and less later in the day, you will feel more awake in the day and fall asleep more easily at night. All just as nature intended.

#4 – When you feel sad

Hug a Tree

When you are feeling down, a great way to pick up your spirits is to reconnect with the natural world around you.

Nature is everywhere, in small pockets in a busy city or in vast acres in the countryside. Just one tree can be enough, if that's all you have.

Hugging a tree is often thought to be a frivolous and pointless exercise, but there is plenty of scientific evidence to support the benefits of tree hugging.

Hugging a tree brings you into close contact with the tree

trunk and, particularly, its bark, which increases levels of oxytocin, a hormone that is boosted by touch, making you feel calmer and more relaxed. To achieve oxytocin release, you need to hug the tree for a minimum of 25 seconds.

Hugging trees also decreases cortisol levels, which reduces feelings of stress and anxiety and even lowers your chance of having a heart attack by slowing your heart rate and reducing your blood pressure.

Even the characteristic scent of a pine tree can have extra benefits when you inhale it. Pine and spruce trees contain phytoncides, that familiar forest scent (think Christmas trees), which have fragrances like essential oils, including lavender and frankincense, both of which are therapeutic and calming.

Phytoncides are antimicrobial and anti-inflammatory. They can boost the immune system. They even have bacteria, virus and cancer-killing properties. Phytoncides include alpha pinene and limonene which can have hugely beneficial effects on your body, mind and spirit.

We would be in a lot of trouble without trees. They remove carbon dioxide from the atmosphere and convert them to vital oxygen for humans to breathe. Trees also have a steady and enduring presence, which means they represent permanence, giving us feelings of security and reassurance.

With all these benefits, why wouldn't you lift your spirits with such a fast and easy fix as hugging a tree? All you need is a tree and a bit of courage. Don't worry what anyone thinks, just go for it. Close your eyes, breathe deeply and let nature do the rest. You are sure to feel better fast!

Fast Fixes for Mornings

For some people, mornings can be the best time of day and for others they can be the worst.

We are all conditioned to dread Monday mornings the most.

If you are struggling to keep going already and lunchtime seems a long way away, here are some *Fast Fixes* to help you to find some energy, cruise through to lunchtime and supercharge your enthusiasm and commitment for making this a great day.

#5 – When pressure at work makes you feel stressed

Quick Fix for Stressful Moments

When you're feeling particularly stressed and you need a very quick fix, try this exercise.

- Find somewhere quiet for a moment
- Make sure that you are sitting or have something to support you if standing
- Close your eyes
- Start counting down backwards from 10, slowly saying each number out loud. You can do this in your head if you need to, if you are in the presence of other people, but saying it out loud is more helpful

- Keep going with a quiet rhythm until you get to zero. Slow down as you get towards the end
- Remind yourself that you are calm, you can cope and everything is going to be ok
- Repeat if necessary or start at a bigger number next time

You'll be surprised how much this quick and simple exercise can calm you down.

If you feel dizzy while you're carrying out the exercise, sit down or hold on to your support or stop until you feel ok again.

> *Stress is an ignorant state. It believes that everything is an emergency. Nothing is that important.*
> **Natalie Goldberg**

This Fast Fix #5 works because it makes you focus on something you don't normally think about, which stops other distracting thoughts going around and around in your mind.

You'll be surprised how much you have to blink when you open your eyes at the end. It will have distracted you so much that you will have actually forgotten where you are for a moment.

Distraction is a great tool for stress. All you need to do is break the cycle of your thoughts to help you to release yourself from them.

Practice this as often as you can or as often as you need to and you will find it gets easier.

Other things you can count backwards are the alphabet from

Z to A or recite a poem to yourself that you remember from your school days.

You can also find repeating affirmations useful at times like this. It's even worth preparing some in advance and having them written down on paper so that you can repeat them. You can find some positive phrases to say to yourself in Fast Fix #32.

#6 - When you feel overwhelmed

Mindful Meditation

Another one of my personal favourite *Fast Fixes* is mindful meditation. It can be done anywhere at any time, no matter how long you have, and it can help in any situation, whatever the why you need some moments of calm and refocus.

It can be particularly helpful when you feel overwhelmed and just need to stop.

However busy you are, you have always got time for this.

People often think that mediation is some deeply complicated and difficult technique and

> *The time to relax is when you don't have time for it.*
> **Sydney J Harris**

they are put off trying it, which is a shame because it is not only very simple and easy to do and has amazing mental health benefits, but it requires no equipment or special skills and it can be done anywhere and at any time.

TAKE A MOMENT

You just need as little as one minute to meditate. If you do 5 minutes every day it will make you look younger. You will be calmer and more focused on what you need to do next. Do you need more reasons that those to give it a try?

Here is a simple 4-step introduction to mindful meditation that you can do whenever you need a little calm in your day, whatever the reason.

- Find a quiet place to sit
- Get comfortable. You can sit cross legged if you like, but it is just as effective to sit in a chair with your feet flat on the floor. You can even lie down, but be aware that you may fall asleep!
- Close your eyes and concentrate on your breathing. Focus on the in breath and then the out breath. Be aware of the air entering and leaving your body. You may notice that paying attention to your breathing will automatically slow it down

> Try to empty your mind of thoughts, but don't worry if you find this difficult. If your mind wanders, which it will do every few seconds (this is completely normal), gently bring it back to a quiet emptiness. If you do find your mind full of thoughts, try to be detached from them. You can observe them in a curious but detached way. Do not try to engage with them at all. Just let them float on past, as though they have nothing to do with you and they have no relevance to your life, and watch them float away, like passing clouds in the sky

That's all there is to it.

Try to practice this every day, or even several times a day, if you can. Start with just 1 minute and build up to 5 or even 10 minutes at a time.

#7 – When you feel anger rising

Write Down Your Thoughts and Feelings

If you are the kind of person who always has a lot going on in your head, often stuff you would rather not think about, then writing down your thoughts and feelings can be a great way to get them out of your head, leaving you feeling clearer and brighter.

Writing down your thoughts and feelings can allow you to organise and clarify them, especially if they are too private to talk about. You do not need to share them with anyone, your writing can be just for you, to keep safe or destroy later, whichever feels right for you. Write a note to yourself or an email to another person, expressing how you feel.

Scribbling some words down on paper, typing them into your phone or tablet or speaking them into a voice to text app are all great options. Whichever you choose, it should feel natural and easy, so you can express yourself freely.

Whatever or however you write, it is just for you so you don't need to worry about making it perfect. You can write quickly, just as your thoughts come. Reading it back later, or maybe the next day, can also be a helpful way to put the thoughts and feelings aside, giving you some distance from them.

This technique can be especially useful if you are feeling angry, upset or resentful, especially towards another person. Writing down what you would like to say to them can be a really good outlet for those uncomfortable feelings you dare not speak about. You may know you will never say those things or send them the note or email, but just getting the things down can help to release you from the feelings so you can move past them.

Next time you feel anger rising or your head is full of stuff going around and around, give your thoughts an outlet so you can let them go and then get on with your day.

#8 – When you are lacking motivation

Get Something Done

If you are a person who likes lists, then you're probably also a person who likes ticking things off and feeling a sense of achievement.

When you are feeling directionless or lacking motivation, or the afternoon slump has hit and you just can't find the energy or enthusiasm to do anything, just doing something to move you forward, however small, can be really uplifting.

Just taking action, getting up and getting on with something, can be a real help. It creates a distraction, burns up that adrenaline and cortisol and makes you feel more positive.

Ticking things off your list gives you a sense of achievement that can give you a real buzz. It also gets that task out of your head, so you can forget about it and move on.

Of course, ticking things off a list relies on having made a list in the first place. If you're lacking focus, one thing you could do is to sit and write a list of all the things you need to do. Don't let it overwhelm you, though, as it's easy to turn this into a negative exercise if you're not careful.

Here are a few things you could do that only take a few moments:

- ✓ Start a to-do list
- ✓ Tidy your desk or closet
- ✓ Read an article in a magazine or ezine
- ✓ Shred some old documents
- ✓ Clear out your inbox
- ✓ Back up your devices
- ✓ Sew on a button or do a small repair
- ✓ Clean the floor
- ✓ Plan the meals for the week
- ✓ List 5 things you can do to improve your health
- ✓ Start a bucket list

- ✓ Find out what's on in your area
- ✓ Write a thank you card
- ✓ Text a friend
- ✓ Declutter a drawer or worktop
- ✓ Learn something new
- ✓ Change your passwords
- ✓ Check your bank balance
- ✓ Just relax (yes, you should put this on your to-do list too)

When you have finished, don't forget to allow yourself to feel a sense of achievement.

Fast Fixes for Lunchtimes

Lunchtimes are your opportunity to take a break, to take some time for yourself, and it really is important that you do just that.

Here are some *Fast Fixes* to help you to unplug and take a break that will really revive you and give you a few minutes of calm in your hectic day, ready to launch into the afternoon. If the day has already got you wound up and stressed, there are some de-stress techniques here too.

#9 – When you feel you need to escape for a while

Revisit a Favourite Book

If you have a favourite book, whether a physical book, one on Kindle or even an audiobook, it can be a great place to go when you are feeling down. The familiarity of a story you love and have visited many times before can be a great comfort, like choosing to spend time with good friends and catching up with their stories.

Alternatively, try downloading the latest book by your favourite author or by an author you have recently discovered and enjoyed and tuck in. Lose yourself for a while in its pages, whether by reading or listening. I often find that an audiobook is easier when you are struggling, because just listening can be less effort than reading and a good narrator can transport you out of your worries and to another place for a while, which provides a really helpful distraction from our worries and thoughts.

Another tip for disappearing into a fictional world is to choose an audiobook, either an old favourite or a new title, pop your headphones on and go out for a walk. The regular beat of your footsteps as you listen to someone telling you a story can be amazingly therapeutic. It transports you into another world, which can be a great distraction from your negative thoughts.

Stephen Fry relates how this method rescued him back from the brink of serious depression, as he spent many hours walking and listening to audiobooks to get him out of his own head and to help him cope with his thoughts.

Sarah Raynor, writing in Psychology Today, says,

Those of us prone to anxiety and depression understand from bitter experience the negative spin cycle of thoughts that accompanies both mental states. Slowing these thoughts enough to read can be hard, if not impossible. Whereas audio does this for you. For those who find it difficult to quieten their inner demons, listening to someone else read aloud can help by replacing negative thoughts with something else.

Audiobooks can also be a great way to calm and relax you before sleep, helping you to get to sleep by quietening a troubled and over busy mind. A familiar book with characters that you know will often enhance this effect, making you feel that you are amongst friends.

Next time you are feeling down and cannot find a way to escape the endless whirl of thoughts in your head, just try this method of escape and see if it helps you too.

#10 – When you need to make time for yourself

Make a Brew

Tea is an incredibly calming drink. It can lift your spirits, calm you down and refresh you, all in one go.

It has been used for centuries as a calming and comforting ritual in many different cultures.

TAKE A MOMENT

> *If you are cold, tea will warm you;*
> *if you are too heated, it will cool you;*
> *if you are depressed, it will cheer you;*
> *if you are excited, it will calm you.*
>
> **William Gladstone**
> **British Prime Minister**

Tea contains L-theanine which promotes gentle relaxation, creating a state of quiet, mindful tranquility, whilst also maintaining focus and alertness. It also reduces the stress hormone cortisol.

It's no wonder we reach for tea when things are not going well.

It's not just the drink itself that's calming. There's a mindful way of drinking it that can help to calm and settle you too. Why not try it for yourself?

- Take your time to choose a type of tea and enjoy its aroma as you spoon it into the teapot. There are so many varieties of tea to choose from, so be brave and try a new one every now and then
- Listen to the water bubbling as the kettle boils
- Watch the tea change colour as it brews
- Choose a favourite cup or mug
- Enjoy the aroma of the tea before you take your first sip
- Notice the taste of the tea as you sip it slowly
- Feel the warmth as it slips down. How does it make you feel?

> If your thoughts wander, bring them back to the tea and its flavour and the pure pleasure of taking time to sit quietly

As well as its calming and reassuring properties, tea also has a host of physical benefits too.

- ✓ high in polyphenols, a type of antioxidant, which protect against aging and the effects of pollution
- ✓ antioxidants also protect you against inflammation and cancer
- ✓ reduces your chances of suffering a heart attack or stroke by keeping your arteries clean and preventing clogging. A study in the Netherlands found that drinking 2 or 3 cups of black tea a day can reduce your chances of suffering a fatal heart attack by 70%
- ✓ contains phytochemicals that protect your bones
- ✓ improves your immune system so it can fight off infection
- ✓ contains fluoride and tannins that protect your teeth (but don't add sugar!)
- ✓ contains less caffeine than coffee. Caffeine can be over-stimulating, giving you the jitters and keeping you awake. Tea can be enjoyed at any time of day

With all these great benefits, you don't need to be feeling down to enjoy a cup of calming tea. Whenever you feel you need to take a break and allow yourself a little me-time, put the kettle on, relax and enjoy all the benefits tea has to offer.

#11 – When you wonder why you should bother

Write a Gratitude Journal

Writing down your thoughts and feelings can be a great way to get rid of your feelings when you are having a bad day. You can also use the same technique to create a daily journal in a more positive way.

When you are writing down or recording your thoughts, you do not have to stick to the bad stuff. You can also record all the good things that happened. Try listing all the things you are grateful for and all the things that are good in your life. You can develop this into a daily gratitude journal to keep and look back on, like a diary.

Reminding yourself of all the things that are good in your life can help to lift your mood, not just in the moment, but in general too. Once you start to think about the things you have in your life that make a difference and for which you are grateful, your overall happiness will increase.

Make it a daily habit to spend a few minutes just thinking about why you are lucky and what you appreciate about your life.

If you are stuck for something to write, here are a few ideas to get you started.

- ✓ Remember that you are lucky to be alive at all. Life is a miracle and every day is a bonus
- ✓ You are lucky to have been born into the relative wealth and comfort of western society. There are much more difficult places to be born and to live
- ✓ You are warm, comfortable, have a roof over your head, food to eat and you have friends and family who care about you
- ✓ You are largely free to choose the life you want to live
- ✓ There are always people having a worse day than you

Being grateful can also be expressed by writing to someone and thanking them for something they did for you. Write a thank you letter for a gift or favour received, or just because someone was there to support you when you need it. Studies show that doing this actually makes people feel more grateful and that feeling can persist over time.

No matter how stressed, anxious, angry or fed up you are feeling right now, there is always something to look forward to and something to be grateful for.

#12 – When the day seems too long already

Have a Nap

When you are feeling low or tired or the day just seems to have lasted forever already, sometimes all you need to pick you up is 10 minutes of total unplugging.

A short, power nap can help to boost your mood, levels of alertness, short-term memory, focus and concentration. It can be especially beneficial if you didn't sleep well the night before or if you are generally sleep-deprived.

- Find somewhere quiet and private, preferably somewhere you can lie down. It will help even more if it is dark
- Your body temperature may drop a little when you nap, so make sure you have a blanket or an extra layer to hand
- Turn off all your devices so you can have a complete break without fear of interruption
- If you think you might fall asleep for longer, set an alarm first
- Close your eyes, take some deep, slow breaths and let your mind drift away

Researchers at Flinders University showed that 10 minutes is the perfect length for a nap. It scored higher for how quickly it makes you feel better and how long-lasting the effects were than naps that were either longer or shorter in duration.

Try not to nap for longer than 15 to 20 minutes or you may

reach the deep sleep part of the sleep cycle, which may make you feel groggy, disorientated or even more drowsy when you wake up.

Don't nap too late in the day or it may reduce your chances of a good night's sleep later.

A nap will not just refresh you at the time. The good news is that napping has benefits beyond just the obvious and immediate ones. Clinical studies have shown that people who nap regularly have a 37% reduction in their risk of mortality due to heart disease and even for people who only nap occasionally the risk reduction is 12%.

> *Almost everything will work again if you unplug it for a few minutes, including you.*
> **Anne Lamontt**

A study at the University of Dusseldorf showed that even just 6 minutes of sleep triggers enhanced memory recall, which suggests that the actual onset of sleep may initiate memory consolidation processing. This effect is maintained even if you wake up after 6 minutes, so even a 6-minute nap will do you good.

The research supports the idea of napping for a short time when you feel the need and there's no down side. Take a break for yourself – 10 minutes will be perfect. Unplug yourself from everything, just for a while, and you will soon feel refreshed and ready to go again.

Part 2 – 33 Fast Fixes to Relax, Restore and Refocus

Connecting with nature can be a great way to realign our perspective and remind ourselves of what is important.

Next time you are feeling down, try getting up and simply taking yourself outside. Take some deep and calming breaths and experience the fresh air and how it makes you feel. Look around you, take in the sounds around you. Just enjoy being outside and you will soon feel calm returning.

Fast Fixes for Afternoons

Afternoons are a challenge for many people. There is the familiar afternoon slump when we tend to crash and run out of energy around mid-afternoon. Our energy and focus can take a dive and we need some help to motivate us and get us going again.

This can be particularly difficult if you are by yourself, with no incentive from the people around you, such as if you work from home or are home taking care of your family.

It can also be a time when the day is starting to get to you and you need a way to unwind and calm down from the pressures and expectations of the day and of other people.

Here are some *Fast Fixes* to calm you down, to help you find your peace and to give you a lift to get you going again.

#14 – When you are finding it hard to keep going

Stretch It Out

When you have been sitting for too long, especially at work, it will help you to feel better if you take a short break and do some stretches.

Stretching makes you feel good, so it is a great *Fast Fix*. It is calming and refreshing, as well as reducing any stiffness you may feel from sitting. It really helps when you are feeling stuck, physically and mentally.

I personally love this one. I find it always makes me feel better physically and mentally, plus it makes me feel optimistic and ready to move on to whatever comes next in my day.

You can stretch your neck, shoulders and arms sitting down or, better still, if you can, get up and stretch out your back, waist, thighs, calves and ankles. All stretching will increase blood flow to the muscles and make you feel energised.

Part 2 – 33 Fast Fixes to Relax, Restore and Refocus

Here are some stretches you can try in just a few minutes.

These stretches are easy and safe for most people but, if you are unsure, please do take medical advice before trying them.

- ➢ Forward Stretch – Stand up straight. Slowly bend forward as far down as you can, aiming your head towards your knees. When you get to the bottom of the stretch, wrap your arms around your legs as far as you can and pull yourself in a little closer. You may not be able to reach that far at first, but this is one that you will find gradually gets easier the more you do it. Hold the posture and count slowly to 10. Return to a standing position. Repeat twice more
- ➢ Neck Reliever Head Roll – You can do this sitting or standing. Allow the head to fall gently forwards, then roll the head to the left side, then back so you are looking upwards, then round to the right, then back to the forwards position again. Repeat in the opposite direction. Repeat twice more in each direction
- ➢ Side Stretch – Stand up straight with your hands hanging by your sides. Lean over to your left, gently moving your left hand down the outside of your thigh to the outside of your knee, or further if you can. Return to a standing position. Repeat to the right. Then repeat the whole sequence twice more
- ➢ Spinal Twist – Lie flat on the floor (or on the bed) with your arms outstretched to each side. Bend your left knee and place the foot flat on the floor. Roll your left knee to the right and then move your lower leg across your right leg and lie it flat on the floor so

TAKE A MOMENT

> your hips are twisted towards the right. Look left towards your left hand and feel the stretch through your midriff. Count slowly to 10. Return to the starting position and repeat to the other side
> Cat stretch – Start on all fours. Curve the centre of your back upwards, so you are arching it like a cat stretching and allow your head to drop forwards and down. Count slowly to 5. Then flatten your back and raise your head up, making your back hollow. Count slowly to 5. Repeat this movement 4 more times. If you prefer, you can do this as a continuous, slow and controlled movement without the pauses

You should feel refreshed, revived and ready to get back to whatever you were doing.

#15 – When you need to concentrate and focus

Take a Power Walk

Walking can help with so many different troublesome moods.

When you are feeling tired or need a refresh, try going for a walk. Walking can be great if you are suffering from the afternoon slump when your energy has dropped

If you're in the office, walking up and down a few flights of stairs can produce the same effect, but get outside if at all possible as the fresh air will also help.

Walking is also an ideal antidote for times when you are

wound up, angry or stressed. Any kind of walk will help, but a power walk is even better than a quiet stroll. Walk with powerful, energetic steps and use your arms as well as your legs. The more you power, the more hormones you use up, which makes it ideal for times when you are feeling stressed or wound up and your adrenaline levels are high.

If you have too much going on in your mind, try putting some headphones on and listen to some music or an audiobook while you walk. Audiobooks can be a great distraction from your thoughts, so this works well when you have things going around in your mind that you would rather forget.

> *A vigorous five-mile walk will do more good for an unhappy but otherwise healthy adult than all the medicine and psychology in the world.*
> **Paul Dudley White**

Rumination is never a good idea because it doesn't solve any problems, it just makes you feel worse. Walking and listening can get you out of your own thoughts.

It doesn't matter what you listen to. Fiction can take you off to another world but nonfiction can be just as helpful and absorbing, so give both a try.

Walking is one of my favourite ways to deal with any challenge. It gets you going, calms you down, gives you time to reflect, allows you to escape, takes very little time, can be done anywhere, it is always available and it's free!

#16 – When you feel wired

Using Exercise to Relieve Restless Energy and Stress

Even though there is rarely any real threat to us in our lives, our bodies react to stress by giving us a massive spike in adrenaline and cortisol. Our primaeval response is to see a stressor as a life-threatening situation where we need to react quickly to keep us safe.

These two hormones provide a huge boost of energy in what your body regards as a moment of panic, fear and danger. You react as though you have suddenly seen a lion that is about to pounce on you and you need to run away very quickly. The sudden release of adrenaline and cortisol gives you the energy boost you need to do that.

Part 2 – 33 Fast Fixes to Relax, Restore and Refocus

Our response is meant to be there to save our lives in an emergency. But in everyday life, when we have an adrenaline and cortisol spike for a reason that is not life threatening or dangerous, we need to find a way to get rid of the excess hormones in our system.

Quick aerobic exercises to fast-burn adrenaline and cortisol include going for a short power walk, run up and down the stairs a few times, jog on the spot for a couple of minutes, do a few jumping jacks or do some energetic cleaning in the house. Some people find housework very therapeutic, with the added bonus of getting the cleaning done!

Exercise is also well-known for making us feel good. Physical activity not only takes your mind off your worries but it also promotes the release of endorphins, the feel-good neurotransmitters that create the sense of euphoria and wellbeing many people feel after a workout, which is also known as *the runner's high*.

Regular exercise can reduce your stress overall. Adding regular exercise into your daily routine will help reduce the occurrence of adrenaline spikes in general.

Taking regular exercise contributes to your overall health, getting you fitter, increasing your metabolism and reducing your weight. Exercise also contributes to positive mental health and an overall feeling of wellbeing.

Next time you are under stress and you feel like leaping up with a burst of energy, remember that this is just your body reacting exactly as it should, however inappropriate it may seem to be. If you get moving with some short energetic activity, you will quickly use up the excess chemicals in your system and you will soon find yourself feeling much calmer.

TAKE A MOMENT

#17 – When you feel anxious or stressed

Using Acupressure Points to Relieve Stress and Anxiety

Acupressure is a safe, noninvasive, traditional Chinese therapy that uses the same meridian points as acupuncture but without the needles. This means you can either seek treatment from a practitioner or you can treat yourself.

There are a number of theories as to why it works. It is generally thought that it releases blocked energy and allows energy to flow freely through the body. Some people think it stimulates the release of endorphins and others think it affects the autonomic nervous system. It is possible that it actually does all of these.

The acupressure points, or acupoints, occur where the meridian lines are closest to the surface of the skin. Each acupoint has a different sensation and a different effect on the body, depending on where the acupoints are located.

A study published in *Neuroscience Letters* in 2009 showed that specific acupoints can have a therapeutic effect for chronic stress-related issues such as anxiety, depression and post-traumatic stress disorder (PTSD).

If you are feeling stressed, anxious and exhausted, here are 5 quick pick-me-up acupressure points that can really help. You can do them discreetly at your desk at work, at home or wherever you are.

Each exercise only takes a couple of minutes. You can choose to do one or two of them when you feel you need them or you can do them all, in the sequence suggested below, in

Part 2 – 33 Fast Fixes to Relax, Restore and Refocus

only 10 minutes.

These exercises are best done sitting, or preferably lying, if possible, but you can do them anywhere and at any time.

The final acupoint below is a perfect **2-minute Superpower Whole-Body Lift** for your mind, body and spirits. If you only have 2 minutes, this is the one to do.

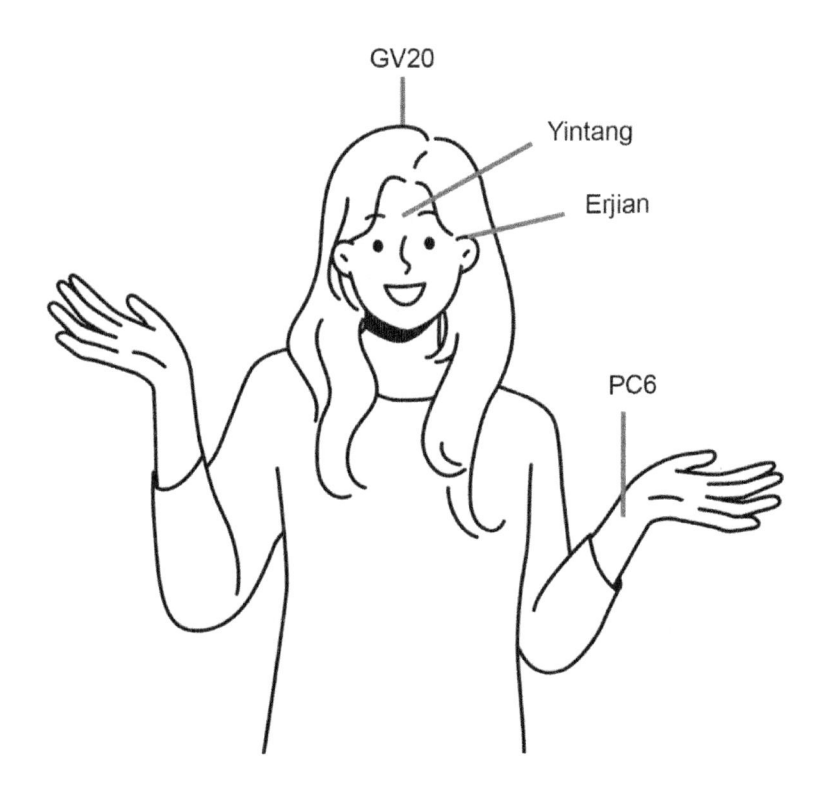

GV20
Yintang
Erjian
PC6

➤ *Yintang for Relaxation* – This point is located midway between your eyebrows. It is great for helping to promote calmness when you are feeling anxious or stressed. Place your middle finger between your eye-

brows and exert a little pressure for 2 minutes. While you do this, concentrate on your breathing and allow yourself to fully relax
- *GV20 for Calm* – This point is located on the top of your head. Imagine drawing a line from one ear to the other over the top of your head and the midpoint on that line is the GV20 point. Apply a little pressure or massage the point for a couple of minutes to help you to feel calm when under pressure or when you are feeling a rising panic
- *Erjian for Stress Reduction* – This point is located right at the top of the ear, on the highest point of the curve. Squeeze the point between your thumb and forefinger for 2 minutes. It can be really helpful for reducing stress and is also good for blood pressure relief, especially if you feel you have reached boiling point and need to calm down
- *GB34 for Confidence and Courage* – This point is located in the depression to the outside just below your knee. Place your middle finger in the centre of the top of your shin bone, just below the knee joint, and

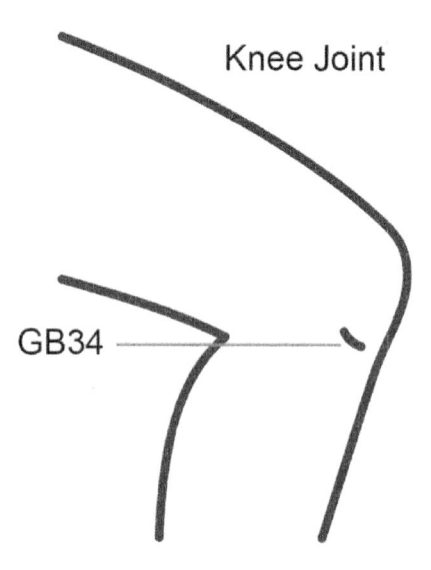

slide it towards the outside of your knee until you feel it drop from the hard, bony surface into a soft dip and you have found the correct place. Apply a little pressure or massage the point for 2 minutes. It will help you to feel brave and give you the power to decide on your next move

> *PC6 for a Superpower Whole-Body Lift* – This point is located in the centre of the wrist, three fingers width down from where your hand and wrist meet. Place your thumb in the crease between the two tendons and apply a little pressure. It can help to apply a steady counter pressure with your forefinger on the other side, as though you are squeezing the thumb and forefinger gently together. PC6 is a Superpower point that can have benefits for the whole body, plus it will give your spirits a lift

Give each of these a try. You will soon find which ones work for you. They are quick and easy to do, so you can turn to them whenever you need.

#18 – When you feel tired and achy

Give Your Neck and Shoulders a Break

Tension in the neck and shoulders is extremely common. It usually occurs as a result of strain to the neck and shoulder muscles caused by prolonged tension. This is often caused by keeping the head and neck in once place for too long without changing position.

TAKE A MOMENT

Modern work from home lifestyles, increased screen time for students and the Covid pandemic have changed the way we carry out our daily work. With so many of us now working from home, we often spend hours sitting at computer screens without moving very much.

The same can also happen if you are absorbed in watching a box set or a movie where you concentrate for an hour or several hours without getting up.

When we look at the computer screen, a TV or a device for long periods, our heads stay in one place for too long, causing tension which creates tightness or can even lock the neck. This creates trigger points, or knots, in specific spots that feel stiff or sore.

To release triggers in your neck and shoulders:

- Find the sore spots (this should be fairly easy)
- Press into the trigger points with your fingers
- Massage the spot with very small movements whilst maintaining the downward pressure (it is unlikely you will press too hard or do any damage)
- Repeat for 1 minute per spot, or longer if needed
- Find the next trigger point
- Repeat as many times a day as necessary

Longer term solutions to neck and shoulder tightness include:

- ✓ Set up a more posture friendly workstation – make sure your chair has arm rests and is adjusted to suit the height of the desk or consider a standing desk solution

Part 2 – 33 Fast Fixes to Relax, Restore and Refocus

- ✓ Look away from your computer screen or device for 1 minute every 20 minutes
- ✓ Do regular stretches to release tension build up
- ✓ Take regular breaks when you get up and move around

Being aware is important and the more you can do to avoid sitting in the same position for too long, the less problems you will have but, if the problem persists, make sure to book a visit to your doctor to get it checked out.

Fast Fixes for Evenings

Evenings are our chance to unwind from the day's challenge. For some people, it means a chance to relax, to watch TV or spend time with friends and family, or maybe to spend time on a hobby or interest.

It is also a time when we need to start to unwind and chill out ready for a good night's rest.

If you are struggling to let go of a build-up of stress and tension, here are some *Fast Fixes* to help you to relax and let go of the day.

#19 – When you can't unwind

Using Emotional Freedom Technique (EFT) for Instant Calm

Emotional Freedom Technique (EFT), also known as tapping or psychological acupressure, is an alternative method of relieving stress and tension, both physical and mental. It can be very helpful for people who suffer from negativity, anxiety, depression or post-traumatic stress disorder (PTSD).

Tapping is very calming. It can be a great way to provide a *Fast Fix* when you are feeling stressed.

It works in a similar way to traditional Chinese acupressure in that it uses the meridian points where energy flow reaches

TAKE A MOMENT

the surface of the skin. These pathways help to balance the energy flow through the body. EFT involves tapping on the points rather than using pressure.

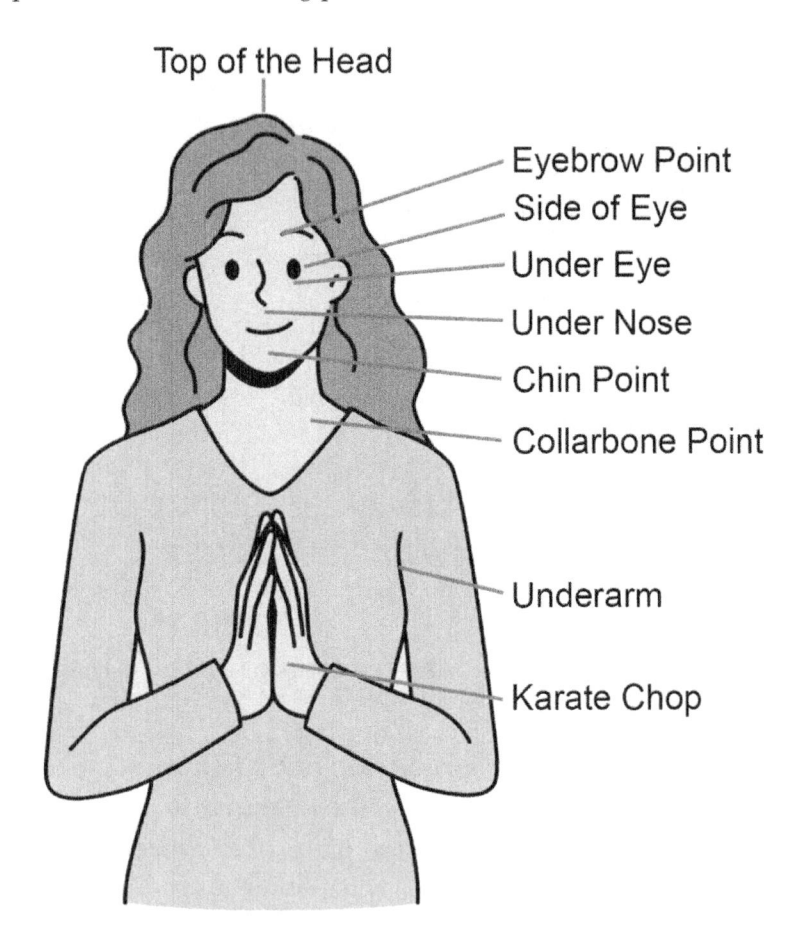

- Top of the Head
- Eyebrow Point
- Side of Eye
- Under Eye
- Under Nose
- Chin Point
- Collarbone Point
- Underarm
- Karate Chop

The nine main EFT tapping points include:

- ✓ Karate Chop (side of the hand)
- ✓ Eyebrow Point (EB)

- ✓ Side of Eye (SE)
- ✓ Under Eye (UE)
- ✓ Under Nose (UN)
- ✓ Chin Point (CP)
- ✓ Collarbone Point (CB)
- ✓ Underarm (UA)
- ✓ Top of the Head (TH)

Here is a short tapping routine that you can use anytime you feel you need a little help.

> Start by identifying and accepting what is bothering you
> Focus your mind on the issue you are dealing with, i.e. what is making you feel stressed
> Work through the tapping points, one at a time
> Use two fingers side by side to tap rhythmically – normally 7 to 9 taps on each point is enough to give you relief
> Tapping on the meridian points while thinking about the cause of your stress in a calm and accepting way helps to rebalance the body's energy

Tapping is quick, easy, painless, noninvasive and cost-free and can be carried out anywhere.

Studies have shown that EFT may have wide-ranging benefits, including reducing stress and anxiety, diminishing food cravings, helping with weight loss and improving focus and concentration.

Even if you have never used EFT before, give it a try. You will soon find yourself feeling calmer and more positive.

#13 – When you feel closed in

Get Outside

With our busy and often office-based lifestyles, it is all too easy to overlook the very valuable resource that is freely available and free to access – outside space. Even if you live in the middle of a city, there is always green space not far away.

How many times have you got to the end of the day and suddenly realised that you didn't actually step outside today?

There are many studies that show the benefits of getting outdoors. Being outside in nature has been shown to be relaxing and calming, reducing stress levels, muscle tension, blood pressure and heart rate, improving focus and concentration, boosting creativity and productivity, supporting quality sleep and helping to combat anxiety and depression.

Not only that, but spending time outdoors increases our overall sense of wellbeing. It lifts our mood and makes us feel more awake and more alive.

That's a lot of benefit for something that is so simple to do and that can be fitted into anyone's day so easily.

Exercising outdoors has added benefits too. It burns up calories. Exercising outdoors has been shown to make the body work harder to balance carbon dioxide levels and requires the body to consume more oxygen, both of which use energy, resulting in a higher calorie burn.

TAKE A MOMENT

#20 – When your mind is going around and around

Look to the Stars

Here's the simplest idea you can possibly have for feeling better in an instant.

This is my favourite *Fast Fix* of all, because it's super quick and easy, you can do it anytime and anywhere and it is so powerful that it works every time, no matter what mood you are in or how you are feeling.

Why not try it right now?

When you're feeling down, tired or need refreshing, try the **STARS** Exercise.

Here's how:

- ➢ **S**top – Stand still wherever you like. Correct your posture and find your balance
- ➢ **T**ip your head back, lift your chin and look straight up above you
- ➢ **A**lert – Open your eyes wide
- ➢ **R**elax – Breathe deeply and slowly as you continue to look up
- ➢ **S**mile
- ➢ Continue to breathe slowly and deeply for as long as you need

It doesn't matter where you're standing, as you can do this anywhere, but if you're outside, it's a lot easier and you'll get more from the exercise. But you can do it inside too, or anywhere you like.

If you are outside then look up at the passing clouds or at the stars in the night sky, depending on what time of day it is. Just stand and watch in wonder at the magnitude and enduring timelessness of nature.

Looking at the stars can make this exercise even more effective. There is something about stars in the night sky that makes us feel a sense of wonder at the universe and our place in it, which is calming and gives us a sense of perspective.

Why does this work?

This posture opens your airways and allows you to breathe more deeply, so you are taking in more oxygen. Deep breaths are calming and focusing. Opening your eyes wide allows more light to enter and land on your retina, which improves your mood. Looking at the clouds or the stars help you to gain perspective and to reconnect you to your place in the universe. Overall, the exercise allows you to pause and forget everything else going on in your life right now.

Once you are used to this exercise, you can take it further by leaning back a little further and lifting your neck back so it's level with your spine. It might help to lean back against something like a nearby tree or a gate or a wall. Be careful not to get dizzy or lose your balance. You will find that it has a very calming and centering effect.

> Dwell on the beauty of life. Watch the stars, and see yourself running with them.
>
> **Marcus Aurelius**

You'll be amazed at how effective something so simple can

be. You will soon find yourself calm, refreshed and more connected.

#21 – When life feels hard going

Find Someone to Talk to, Even If It is Yourself

In a recent study as part of the *American Perspectives Survey* (2021), the number of close friends that people say they have has fallen in the last 25 years from 10 or more to less than three and 13% of people say they do not have a close friend at all.

Friends on social media do not count as friends in the same way as traditional types of friendships because what is presented on social media is often an idealised and edited version of people's lives in which they rarely post about their real problems. We also tend to be less connected to those we only contact online.

It seems that, in this age of social isolation, we are finding it increasingly difficult to find people to talk to or to confide in and we have no one to turn to for advice when we are feeling down.

What do you do when you have had a bad day and you need someone to talk through the things that are on your mind if there is no one available?

Writing down your thoughts in a diary or journal in the evening can be a great way to think through and rid yourself of the bad stuff that has happened during your day. Pouring out how you feel on paper can be a valuable way to talk it out when there is no one to listen.

Part 2 – 33 Fast Fixes to Relax, Restore and Refocus

If you have never written a diary or journal before, you may be surprised to find how easy and therapeutic it can be.

- Start by writing down what happened in your day and, more importantly, how you feel about it. You could write as though you are talking to a friend or even just write to yourself
- You can be as honest as you like, because it is completely private and only you are ever going to read it. In fact, if it has done its job in letting you vent out your feelings, then you do not even need to read it yourself again in the future, unless you want to

- How you record your thoughts is a personal choice. You can use a simple notebook or a specifically designed journal in which you can write by hand, you can type into a document on your PC or device or you can use a voice recorder or voice to text app, which will transcribe your speech into text
- Sometimes just recording your feelings by saying them out loud is enough but, if you prefer, you can paste the transcription into a document to edit and read back, which is usually much faster than writing or typing
- Whatever way you choose, what is most important is to allow yourself the freedom to be honest and open
- Reading or listening to your words afterwards, either the same evening or the next day, allows you to have some distance and perspective. Try to think what you would say to a friend if it was them telling you how they were feeling. What would you advise them?

Making your diary or journal a daily habit can be very helpful, even if you only spend 5 or 10 minutes a day recording how you felt about your day. If things have gone well, that may be all you need, but if things have gone badly, then talk for as long as you need to get it all out of your system. You will be surprised at how cleansing it is to document your feelings and then let them go.

Writing or recording your thoughts can also help you to clarify how you feel, which can enable you to start seeing how you can go forward. You might decide to take action as a result, or just to allow your feelings to settle and then let them go.

Part 2 – 33 Fast Fixes to Relax, Restore and Refocus

You know yourself and what works for you. Go with whatever feels right. You may soon find you are able to deal with the ups and downs of life with more confidence and self-belief.

Fast Fixes for Bedtime

Sleep is essential, but modern lifestyles often encourage us to believe that it is something we can compromise rather than prioritise.

If you are struggling to get to sleep or to have a good night's rest, if you find you wake often and find it hard to get back to sleep again, if everything is just going around in your head or you are worrying about tomorrow, try these *Fast Fixes* to relax and find a sense of calm.

#22 – When you feel lost

Look Inside and Reconnect

Whenever you are feeling lost and needing to find your way again, the best place to start is some inner reflection. Or, better still, start with some inner connection.

> *You have to believe in yourself when no one else does – that makes you a winner right there.*
> **Venus Williams**

This is also a great exercise to do at the end of a busy day, when everything from your day is still buzzing around in your head.

- Find a quiet place to be, somewhere you feel relaxed and where there is the minimal amount of external distraction

- Get comfortable, however that is for you. You can choose to sit or lie down

- Close your eyes and take a slow, deep breath in. Then breathe out even more slowly, making sure you take longer to breathe out than you did to breath in. Try counting to 5 slowly as you breathe in and counting to 7 slowly as you breathe out. Do this a few times

- Become aware of your body and how it feels. Notice how each part of your body feels. Are you tense and tight, does anything ache, can you relax more into the chair, the bed or the floor? Work on each part of the body, starting with your head and working down. I always find relaxing the tiny muscles around the corners of my eyes is a great place to start as it relaxes your whole face

- Now allow your mind to clear of clutter. Whatever has happened in your day, just let it go. Let the drama of the day seep away. You are done with it for now. You are unplugging from the mains

- Even if there are unresolved things for you to worry about, remined yourself you can sleep on them, allow your subconscious to mull them over during the night and you will be able to worry about them a bit less tomorrow. You may even find that an answer of some kind will be there ready for you when you wake

- Now let yourself just be. Feel what it is to just be

alive, with no thoughts of the day or of tomorrow, just what there is in this moment. Just you, relaxed, sitting or lying still with nothing that you need to be concerned with in this moment

Practice this sense of just being, of just being alive, as often as you can. Let it fill you. Let it pervade every part of you, enriching you with a sense of peace and wellbeing

This is where you can find your true self. It is a place of sanctuary, calmness and truth you can return to whenever you need to.

#23 – When you feel depressed

Sleep it Off

It's easy to mistake tiredness for sadness, because they can sometimes feel very similar. Real sadness penetrates deep into your soul, but so too does fatigue on occasions.

Sleep can be a real help for both these problems, especially if you have mistaken tiredness for sadness. Sometimes a few early nights can be a real boost to the way you are feeling. It is worth a try to see if it helps.

Dr. Alex Dimitriu, a psychiatrist and sleep medicine specialist in California, USA, says. "A lot of times it can be hard to know your own feelings, and too often in my work, people with fatigue end up thinking they are depressed."

There is a difference between feeling sleepy, when you just feel the need to go to sleep and rest, and fatigue, which can cause low mood, hopelessness, reduced energy, poor motivation and the inability to concentrate.

There is no doubt that lack of sleep contributes to low mood. When you are tired, you are more likely to feel angry, frustrated, anxious or depressed. If you are suffering from any of these on a regular basis, try looking after yourself a little better, nurture and care for yourself more than usual and give yourself a lot more opportunity to rest. Sometimes you can just sleep off sadness, because it really is tiredness in disguise.

Sleep is not, of course, a substitute for getting proper medical help. If your low moods persist, please do seek professional advice, either through your GP, a support group or a therapist. There are lot of people out there who can help and they will all be experienced in understanding how you are feeling. You do not need to struggle on alone.

We all need a bit of help sometimes and there is nothing wrong with that. Remember that asking for help is not giving up, it is showing courage and refusing to give up.

Part 2 – 33 Fast Fixes to Relax, Restore and Refocus

#24 – When you are unsettled and can't sleep

Own a Place of Sanctuary

Sometimes, when things are going wrong in our lives, it's useful to have a place to escape to. This may be because you are facing challenges at work or at home, in your relationship or your family life, or it could just be thoughts in your head that you're finding difficult to let go.

For times like these, having your own place of sanctuary, a place of comfort and familiarity where you can be in control, somewhere you can go when things feel overwhelming, can be very valuable.

It can be a place that you know or have visited that is associated with happy memories or it can be a place you have invented for yourself, somewhere that you create and develop over time.

Your place of sanctuary is a place where everything is how you would like it to be. It should be a perfect place where you feel safe and enjoy spending time. Most importantly, it is available for you to visit in your mind whenever you need.

> *Within you, there is a stillness and a sanctuary to which you can retreat at any time and be yourself.*
>
> **Herman Hesse**

Many people find calm and peace in nature, so a place of sanctuary could be an empty beach where you can relax in

TAKE A MOMENT

the sun, a mountaintop retreat or a pine forest with its invigorating fragrance. Maybe you are near to water, beside a river or lake or standing next to a waterfall. Or perhaps you prefer a cosy sitting room with a blazing fire, the logs crackling as the reflection from the flames flicker up the walls.

Or maybe, for you, your happy place is in a full stadium, watching your favourite team score the final goal of the season that wins the championships. Or maybe it's taking part in a sporting activity, imagining yourself winning a gold medal at the Olympics in your favourite sport.

Whatever makes you happy.

Whenever you are feeling stressed and need to escape, try the **CALM** Technique to bring you back to a good place.

Hint: You might like to set a timer to do this exercise, if you think you're likely to drift off and lose track of time, or even fall asleep if you get super-relaxed.

- ➤ **C**lose your eyes and gradually take yourself to your place of sanctuary, allowing yourself to slip into the scene
- ➤ **A**ttend to the present moment. Take in everything about your surroundings. What can you see around you that makes you smile? What peaceful sounds are there, such as birds singing or the rippling of the wind in your hair? What can you smell and taste? What makes you feel relaxed?
- ➤ **L**et it all go. Breathe deeply and slowly and get fully absorbed in the scene
- ➤ **M**e-time. Spend as long as you need. This is your time
- ➤ When you come back to the present time, do so gradually. Give yourself time to readjust to being back in the real world
- ➤ Alternatively, if it is the end of the day, let yourself drift off to sleep. You will find the more relaxed you are, the better sleep you have. If you are using the CALM technique to help you sleep, it is best to choose a calm and quiet place of sanctuary

Remember, your happy place is somewhere you can go whenever you want to or whenever you need to. It's private and it's only yours. You can have it any way you want. You don't have to tell anyone about it.

Why not start developing a place of sanctuary right away, so it is there ready for whenever you need it?

Fast Fixes for Anytime

Life is stressful. We all have times when we feel overwhelmed by the pressures and responsibilities we face in our daily lives.

If you are feeling stressed, anxious, sad, helpless, lonely or at breaking point at any time of day, for any reason, try these *Fast Fixes* to quickly calm and reset your mind and body, so you can find some tranquil moments in the chaos and to give you a renewed belief in life and in the future.

#25 – When you need to calm down

Learn to Breathe

If you've never tried it, you might be surprised just how powerful breathwork can be. We think we know how to breathe because we're alive, but there's so much more to correct breathing than you might think. The therapeutic benefits that learning correct breathing techniques can bring are so great

> *Breathe. Let it go. And remind yourself that this very moment is the only one you know you have for sure.*
>
> **Oprah Winfrey**

that it is well worth spending some time learning how to do it. Once you have understood the basics, practicing regularly will increase the calming effects.

Most people are unaware of how they are breathing, but becoming aware of your breath can help to identify when an anxiety or panic attack is heading your way. When we are stressed, we tend to breath in short, rapid, shallow breaths, based up in the chest. When we are calm and relaxed, we tend to take longer, deeper and slower breaths based in the abdomen (belly) area.

Try this exercise when you're feeling stressed or anxious and need to calm and refocus your mind.

- Find a comfortable position, lying down on your back or sitting upright in a chair with both feet on the floor
- Close your eyes
- Place one hand on your upper abdomen, around your waist area, and the other hand in the centre of your chest
- Breathe normally and try to notice which hand moves upwards the most as you breathe in and out
- If you find you are breathing more in your chest, try moving the breathing down to your abdomen area instead. To do this you need to keep your chest still and allow the air to flow down and fill your abdomen instead. Imagine there is a balloon in your stomach that is filling with air
- Continue to practice, breathing in through your nose and out through your mouth. Notice how your

breathing starts to slow and become deeper and your mind becomes calmer as you relax

Try this exercise whenever you are feeling stressed or anxious and practice regularly, even when you are not stressed.

#26 – When you feel down

Smile, Even When You Don't Feel Like It

Researchers disagreed for many years as to whether smiling actually made you feel better, until a group of researchers at the University of South Australia carried out an experiment involving 120 people (55 men and 65 women).

The participants were asked to smile while holding a pen in between their teeth. This forced their facial muscles to replicate a smile, regardless of how they were actually feeling. This action not only caused the muscles to fake a smile, but it made the participants feel happier and more positive. It seemed that the brain did not distinguish between a

TAKE A MOMENT

real smile and a fake one.

The action of forcing the facial muscles to smile, even without the participants feeling happy enough to smile naturally, tricked the brain into releasing neurotransmitters, including dopamine and serotonin, that created a positive emotional state. The participants only had to paste on a fake smile to feel genuinely happier.

Fernando Marmolejo-Ramos, a human and artificial cognition specialist at the University and the author of the study, concluded that there is a strong link between action and perception. He said, "A 'fake it 'til you make it' approach could have more credit than we expect."

> *Sometimes your joy is the source of your smile and sometimes your smile is the source of your joy.*
>
> **Thích Nhất Hạnh**

Another study by a group at the University of Tennessee, Knoxville and Texas A&M, USA, who looked at almost 50 years of data involving 11,000 participants in 138 countries, agreed that facial expressions do have an impact on how we feel. They concluded that smiling makes people feel happier, scowling makes them feel angrier and frowning makes them feel sadder.

With all that evidence to back it up, forcing yourself to smile, even when you don't feel like it, can put you in a more positive mood by increasing the chemicals that make you feel happier. This must be one of the quickest and easiest ways to pick yourself up.

If you can go beyond a smile, then laughter is a great

medicine because it not only stimulates your muscles, heart and lungs, increasing your intake of oxygen, it also releases endorphins, the feel-good chemical that instantly reduces stress.

Keep practicing, because the more you do it, the easier it becomes.

Smiling has one more great benefit: the more you smile, the more people smile back. Not only does this make your day feel better, it lifts the mood of the people around you too.

#27 – When you need to change your mood

Listen to Music

Music can be a very powerful way to change your mood. Listening to music can not only be fun, but it has real psychological benefits.

Studies have shown that music with a strong beat can change your brainwave function because your brain tunes itself into the rhythm of the beat. A faster rhythm can make you feel more alert and help your concentration and a slower rhythm can help you feel calmer.

Music of different beats can train the brain to adapt its speed more easily when required, meaning that the music is training your brain to be more adaptable to different circumstances. The result is that these positive benefits can last long after you have stopped listening to the music.

Music can quickly make you feel more positive, whatever mood you are in. It can also affect the autonomic nervous system, reducing your heart rate and breathing and making you feel more relaxed.

Your mood should guide to your choice of music to listen to. Choose some soothing tracks to help you to relax or put on something faster and more upbeat to lift your mood and get you moving. If you feel like getting up and dancing, then so much the better.

Music can also be a powerful vehicle to taking you back to places or experiences you have had in the past. If there are special songs that you associate with happy times in your life, then playing these to remind you of those times can also be really helpful at difficult times.

It's a great idea to have some different choices close to hand for those moments when you need some help, particularly when you are alone and there is no one nearby to talk to. You could set up some play lists on your phone in advance, suitable for different moods, so you have them readily to hand for those difficult days.

When you need waking up and motivating or when you need calming down and soothing, music can be a powerful mood changer.

Next time you're feeling down and need a lift or when you are wired and need something to make you relax, try music therapy to give you a *Fast Fix* mood boost.

#28 – When you need comfort and reassurance

Hug a Pet

There are so many great reasons to have a pet. Owning a pet keeps you fit, because they need daily exercise, keeps you focused on a daily routine, promotes a sense of responsibility, provides a feeling of companionship, reduces blood pressure, boosts your immune system, alleviates pain and boosts your mood.

People who regularly interact with animals are said to be 22.7% happier than people who don't.

Studies have shown that hugging your pet regularly reduces stress hormones and promotes the release of the feel-good hormones dopamine and serotonin, both of which make you feel calmer and happier. It also reduces anxiety and depression.

Cuddling your pet for 15 minutes or more also increases levels of oxytocin, the hormone that bonds mothers to their babies, which reduces stress. Cuddling your pet first thing in the morning can be especially good to help you to feel calm and relaxed and to get you into the right frame of mind to face the day ahead.

Likewise, cuddling up at night can be a great way to relax and let go of the stresses of the day before you go to sleep.

Time spent encouraging your pet to play with toys can create a sense of bonding, keep you fit and is also fun!

Pets are entirely non-judgmental, which can be a great comfort when you feel the world is against you or no one understands you. Your pet will always be there to remind you that you are loved, needed and appreciated.

> *Petting, scratching and cuddling a dog could be as soothing to the mind and heart as deep meditation and almost as good for the soul as prayer.*
> **Dean Koontz**

Animals can give a strong sense of comfort and support, which is why they are often used for therapy too. Dogs, cats and even horses are taken into hospitals to give patients a lift through physical contact.

Finally, pets can even increase your lifespan. A study of 2,435 cat owners showed significantly lower risk of death from heart attacks, stroke and stress-related illnesses compared to the 2,000 participants who did not own a cat.

When you are feeling down and need a friend, snuggle up with your pet and let them show you how much you are loved and needed.

#29 - When you feel lonely

Phone or Text a Friend or Family Member

When you are feeling sad or lonely, connecting with someone you know can give you a real boost. Just a few minutes talking to or texting a friend or family member can be enough to restore your mood to a happier place.

It has long been known that making social connections is a vital part of a happy and balanced lifestyle. Your social support network is essential for wellbeing. People who have better relationships and more close friends – the kind you would feel comfortable confiding a problem to – are generally happier than those who don't.

Knowing there are people there you can share things with and who you know will be there for you if you need them, gives us a sense of security and reassurance and reduces the chance of loneliness.

Making social connections has also been shown to be a great boost to wellbeing.

If you are lucky enough to be in closer proximity of your friend or family member so you can be in the same room as them, consider putting the kettle on and sitting down for a chat, or ask for a hug. Hugging has been shown to improve the immune system as well as making us feeling instantly better because we know that someone cares.

It doesn't need to take long. Quality of support rather than quantity can be enough to give you a boost.

If you find it difficult to meet new people, try joining a local

Part 2 – 33 Fast Fixes to Relax, Restore and Refocus

interest group where you can meet people with similar interests.

Remember to make sure your friends and family know that you are there for them too, so they can turn to you when they need some support or advice or just a friendly voice to give them a lift.

#30 – When you feel over tired

Take a Bath or Shower

We all know how refreshing that morning shower can be or how a relaxing soak in the bath or tub can be at the end of a long day, but bathing or showering can be a Fast Fix to help you feel great at any time of day.

When you are feeling over tired, a quick shower can be a really great way to wake you up and help you feel refreshed and ready to tackle whatever is next in your day.

Bathing or showering also have many, less well-known benefits.

Here are some reasons why showering makes us feel great:

- ✓ feeling clean physically is mentally cleansing too
- ✓ helps to make you feel more alert
- ✓ warm water soothes away aches and pains and reduces body temperature, promoting sleep
- ✓ makes you feel more positive and optimistic by stimulating the release of oxytocin, a feel-good hormone that reduces stress and promotes a feeling of relaxation
- ✓ the moving water creates negative ions in the air around you, promoting a feeling of wellbeing

- ✓ the pressure of the water on your skin acts like a massage, relaxing tight muscles and improving your circulation

Here are some reasons why taking a bath makes us feel great:

- ✓ soaking in warm water increases body temperature, making you feel relaxed
- ✓ soaking in a warm bath increases the release of serotonin, the feel-good chemical associated with happiness and wellbeing
- ✓ baths can also reduce depression, anxiety and anger
- ✓ warm water can help to reduce blood pressure, improving heart health. One study involving over 30,000 participants showed that Japanese men who bathed daily had a lower risk of heart disease than those who bathed only once a week
- ✓ makes you feel less lonely because the warm water provides physical warmth and the brain is unable to distinguish this from emotional warmth, which is comforting
- ✓ taking a hot bath can kill bacteria, improve your immune system and relieve the symptoms of cold and flu

Taking a bath or a shower means giving yourself a break and taking time for yourself, which will help you to feel calmer and promotes a feeling of self-care and wellbeing.

With all these mental and physical health benefits, there is literally no downside to taking time to care for yourself with a relaxing bath or an invigorating shower.

TAKE A MOMENT

However you are feeling, take 10 minutes to switch off and have some me-time. No matter which you choose, you will soon be feeling clean, refreshed and ready to return to your day in a calmer and more peaceful state of mind.

#31 - When life seems boring and pointless

Make a Plan

Life is a balance between living in the current moment, taking time to remember the past and planning for the future.

When you are finding life challenging or boring or you lack motivation, one way to shake yourself into a happier mood is to plan something for some future date. This could be a vacation, a day or evening out, a family party, a get together with friends or a meal out with your partner.

Studies show that planning for the future makes you feel more positive and increases your resilience against stressful situations. It makes sense to think that, if you have a lot to look forward to, you are more likely to be able to shrug off immediate concerns by thinking about all you have ahead of you.

It is no coincidence that travel firms have a flood of holiday bookings in January. The Christmas holidays are over, the evenings are dark, the weather is cold and the immediate future can seem depressing.

Planning a summer holiday can give you a focus for something in the future you are excited about. Many people chose to book their next holiday as soon as they return from the last one, making sure they always have something ahead of them to look forward to.

Spend a few minutes thinking about things you would like to do, places you want to visit or goals you dream of achieving.

Ask yourself these questions:
- What goals and ambitions do you have?
- What would it mean to you to achieve your goals and why are they important to you?
- How would you feel when you had succeeded?
- What would you need to do to get started?

TAKE A MOMENT

Action Plan:
- ✓ Make a list of things you would like to do or places you would like to visit
- ✓ Choose one thing from your list
- ✓ Start doing some research on how you would complete that goal
- ✓ Set yourself a deadline for when you are going to achieve it
- ✓ Take the first step

Whatever you plan, big or small, make it something that genuinely fills you with warmth and excitement at the very thought. Even if you only have a few minutes to spare, doing a quick online research for ideas can be enough to give you a boost. You will be amazed at the flood of positive feelings of optimism and happiness that will fill you. Then go and make it happen!

#32 - When you are feeling negative

Positive Self-Talk

When you are feeling negative, anxious or lacking confidence, giving yourself a pep talk can be a real boost.

Self-talk is the inner dialogue we have with ourselves in the endless stream of thoughts that run through our heads all day, every day. It is completely normal.

Self-talk can be positive, negative or somewhere in between the two. More often than not, it is a mixture of all of these. If you tend to look more on the negative side, it is likely that you are imagining your life as being more stressful than it really is, making yourself more anxious and less happy.

There is no doubt that we, as individuals, are genetically inclined to be either more positive or more negative in our general outlook, but this does not mean we are stuck with whatever nature gave us. We can all decide to change the way we talk to ourselves, it just takes a little practice.

There are loads of benefits to positive self-talk. It is no surprise that a positive outlook tends to create a more positive and healthier lifestyle. People who are more positive take better care of themselves, eat more healthily, exercise more and don't smoke or drink to excess.

> *The greatest weapon against stress is our ability to choose one thought over another.*
> **William James**

Positive self-talk also improves our immune system, leads to better cardiovascular health, reduces pain, reduces stress, increases energy and enhances life satisfaction.

What can you do if this doesn't sound like you? How can you change the way you look at life?

Positive self-talk is all about ignoring the inner critic, being kind to yourself and telling yourself that you're ok. When you find you are being overly critical of yourself, try these more positive mantras that you can say to yourself:

- ✓ I can handle this
- ✓ I am allowed to feel what I feel
- ✓ I am not my thoughts
- ✓ Everyone makes mistakes, I can fix this
- ✓ At least I tried and that is enough
- ✓ I learned a lot and I will be better next time
- ✓ I am strong and I can get through this
- ✓ I cannot control what other people think but it is my choice what I think
- ✓ It's ok for me to be who I am
- ✓ I don't need anyone else's approval
- ✓ Life is full of ups and downs but I am still going in the right direction
- ✓ I am good enough
- ✓ I have everything I need within me

Try to see that, in any situation, there are always lots of other ways to look at something. Do not accept what your own thoughts are telling you as being the truth. You can always choose to see things differently.

Looking on the brighter side is something that you need to practice, but it will get easier. The brain is capable of huge degrees of adaptation (called *neuroplasticity*). Keep working on it and you will soon find that you start to see things in a more positive light, without even needing to think about it.

Part 2 – 33 Fast Fixes to Relax, Restore and Refocus

#33 – When you are losing hope

Know It's Not Forever

As with everything in nature, the human body has a reset system that brings the body and mind back to a state of equilibrium.

TAKE A MOMENT

When you are going through tough times, you just need to remind yourself that nothing lasts forever, including the bad stuff.

Remember a time when you were really happy, maybe on your birthday, during a day out with friends or when you had achieved something important in your life. Remember the high you felt. But after a while, you settled back to your normal levels again and the excitement wore off and became a memory, as you got on with your regular life.

This is also true of times when you feel bad, even though it can be hard to think about that at the time. Remind yourself that your body will reset in its own time, so you are back to equilibrium again, if you just give it the space and time to do so.

When you are physically tired, you rest and let your body reset.

When you are mentally challenged, you need to do the same thing. Be kind to yourself. Give your mind a break. Remind yourself that nature will reset.

One way to do this is to use the mantra: *This too will pass.*

Whatever it is that you are going through, it will not last forever. The way you feel now is only temporary and you can, and will, get through it and come out the other side back in equilibrium again.

Your bad mood, your anger, your disappointment, your sadness, they too will pass in time. Just trust that it's going to be ok.

Part 3
Your 30-Day Challenge

Part 3

Part 3 – Your 30-Day Challenge

How are you feeling right now?

How would you like to be feeling in 30 days' time?

Take a few minutes to write down the answers to these two questions. Then give yourself a score out of 10 for each question, where 1 is pretty rubbish and 10 is as amazing as you can imagine being.

Keep your answers safe for now, as you will need them later.

> *Don't take your health for granted. Don't take your body for granted. Do something today that communicates to your body that you desire to care for it. Tomorrow is not promised.*
> **Jada Pinkett Smith**

The following are quick activities or ideas for self-care time. Try to do one each day for the next 30 days.

None of them need to take much time out of your day.

You don't need to do them in the order laid out below, you can choose to do them however and whenever you wish, or add in your own ideas if you prefer.

What's important is to do *something* every day to make a difference, however small, to your health and wellbeing.

Remember, you are important and worth taking care of. You will be a better person for yourself and for others if you take care of yourself right now, as well as looking after your long-term health.

Week 1 – Days 1 to 7

Day 1

Get up early and spend 5 minutes outside in the early morning light before starting your day.

Day 2

Create a place of sanctuary that you can escape to whenever you need, as described in *Fast Fix* 24.

Day 3

Spend 10 minutes practising mindful meditation as explained in *Fast Fix* 6. If you can only do 1-2 minutes at first, that's fine, just keep practising.

Day 4

Make yourself some tea and find a quiet place to read a book for 10 minutes.

Day 5

Try the acupoints in *Fast Fix* 17. Which one helped the most?

Day 6

Write a list of the things you are grateful for in your life.

Part 3 – Your 30-Day Challenge

Day 7

Do something for someone else without expecting anything in return. See how it makes you feel.

Week 2 – Days 8 to 14

Day 8

Listen to some music to give you a lift and dance if you feel like it.

Day 9

Take a lunchtime break and do the neck and shoulder exercises in *Fast Fix* 18.

TAKE A MOMENT

Day 10

Try the EFT techniques in *Fast Fix* 19. Did they help?

Day 11

Make a bucket list of things you would like to do before the end of the year and work out how to do the first one.

Day 12

Smile at someone and make their day. It will lift yours too.

Day 13

At the end of your day, relax with the reconnection exercise in *Fast Fix* 22.

Day 14

Focus on your sleep today. Do the STARS exercise in Fast Fix 20 before having an early night.

Week 3 – Days 15 to 21

Day 15

Start the day with the stretching exercises in *Fast Fix* 14.

Day 16

Make time to catch up with a friend you have not been in touch with for a while. Phone, text or email, whichever is easiest.

Day 17

Treat yourself to a pamper session in the bath or shower. Take as long as you need.

TAKE A MOMENT

Day 18

Practice the breathing exercises in *Fast Fix* 25.

Day 19

Take a 10-minute walk outside during your lunch break.

Day 20

Write down 5 things you like about yourself or 5 achievements you are proud of.

Day 21

Revisit your place of sanctuary that you created on Day 2 (*Fast Fix* 24). See if you can develop it further so you feel more a part of it. Or see how far can you go in creating your perfect dream or ambition?

Week 4 – Days 22 to 28

Day 22

Review the last 3 weeks. Note down the activities you did that helped you the most. Choose your favourite 7 activities and repeat one each day for the next 7 days. You can repeat an activity more than once if you found it particularly helpful.

Day 23

Your favourite activity 1. What do you like about it?

Day 24

Your favourite activity 2. How did this help you?

Day 25

Your favourite activity 3. How did you feel afterwards?

Day 26

Your favourite activity 4. Did this work for you as well as the first time you tried it?

Day 27

Your favourite activity 5. Would you recommend this to a friend?

Day 28

Your favourite activity 6. How could you improve this activity and make it work even better for you?

Week 5 – Days 29 and 30

Day 29

Your favourite activity 7. How calm and relaxed did you feel at the end?

TAKE A MOMENT

Day 30

Review the last 7 days. Did you find when you repeated an activity that it had less benefit, the same benefit or more benefit than when you did it the first time? Can you improve it and make it work better for you?

Choose your top favourite activity to do today. Why do you like it? How does it make you feel?

Tracking Your Progress

An additional way to gain benefit from the 30-Day Challenge is to rate each activity you complete from 1 to 5, where 1 is an activity that didn't really help and 5 is an activity that made you feel great, lifted your mood or gave you renewed energy or focus.

Write down what you did, when (time of day can be a factor) and how it made you feel. This can be a one-word answer, or write more if you want.

You can also track your progress using a tracker you can download from the internet and print out to pin up on your wall or by using a tracker or habit app on your phone or tablet to help you to record and follow your progress.

What Next?

If you have got this far *congratulations*!

I hope you are feeling better, calmer and happier.

Look back to your answers to the two questions you wrote down at the start of the challenge.

Did you achieve what you had hoped?

Which one of the ideas suggested above, or of the ones you added in yourself, did you find the most helpful?

Which made you feel the calmest and most peaceful?

Which made you smile the most?

Going forward, I encourage you to find a way to incorporate some of these into your life every day. You will already know which ones worked for you and which ones you enjoyed doing. If you can turn these into regular habits, you will

TAKE A MOMENT

benefit all the more.

The 30-Day Challenge is just the starting point. It is up to you where you go from here.

One suggestion is to choose your 7 favourite *Fast Fixes* or your 7 favourite activities from the 30-Day Challenge, allocate them to the 7 days of the week and then repeat each one on the same day each week, so that you establish a routine that works for you. Find a schedule that fits around your other responsibilities and commitments and you are more likely to stick to it.

> *There is enough time for self-care. There is not enough time to make up for the life you'll miss by not filling yourself up.*
> **Jennifer Williamson**

Ultimately, what really matters is that you make taking time for yourself a daily priority.

However hard it is and whatever pressures you are under, make sure you prioritise taking at least 10 minutes every day for your self-care.

Remember, you will be no help to anyone else unless you take care of yourself first.

Taking care of yourself and your mental wellbeing is every bit as important as taking care of your body. Your investment in yourself will pay you back a thousand times over, now and in the future.

Part 4
Conclusion

Part 4

Part 4 – Conclusion

Life is hectic and demanding. We all struggle at times. Remember that taking care of yourself, taking a few minutes out of your day just to stop, calm and refocus, will repay you a thousand times over.

When life seems hard going, be kind to yourself. It is all too easy to think you are not working hard enough, not trying hard enough or just not good enough.

We can be our own harshest critics, judging ourselves as falling short in whatever we do.

It isn't easy to learn to appreciate ourselves, especially when people around us don't seem to do the same. But you are your strongest advocate.

> *You have been criticising yourself for years, and it hasn't worked. Try approving of yourself and see what happens.*
> **Louise Hay**

You need to be on your own side. Be your own best friend, because you are the one person you can guarantee will be best friends with you for life.

Finally, if you feel guilty about taking time for yourself, or if you feel that to do so is to be self-indulgent without purpose, then I will leave you with this quote from Berni Sewell:

TAKE A MOMENT

Do what you love as often as you can. Walk in the sun, sit on the beach, lie in the grass. Just because it feels good.

Do it without feeling guilty or beating yourself up for the lack of purpose. Without fear over whether you are important enough, useful enough, influential, significant, or deserving enough.

Because, at the end of the day, purpose can add to your happiness, but it's not a prerequisite for it. You don't need a mission, purpose, a direction for your life to be worth living.

You don't have to justify your existence or prove your worth. Not to your parents or your family; not to your friends, your boss, or society.

Not even to yourself.

Because you **are** *worth personified. You matter. Right here, right now.*

And as long as you enjoy walking your path, no matter how aimlessly, your life has meaning.

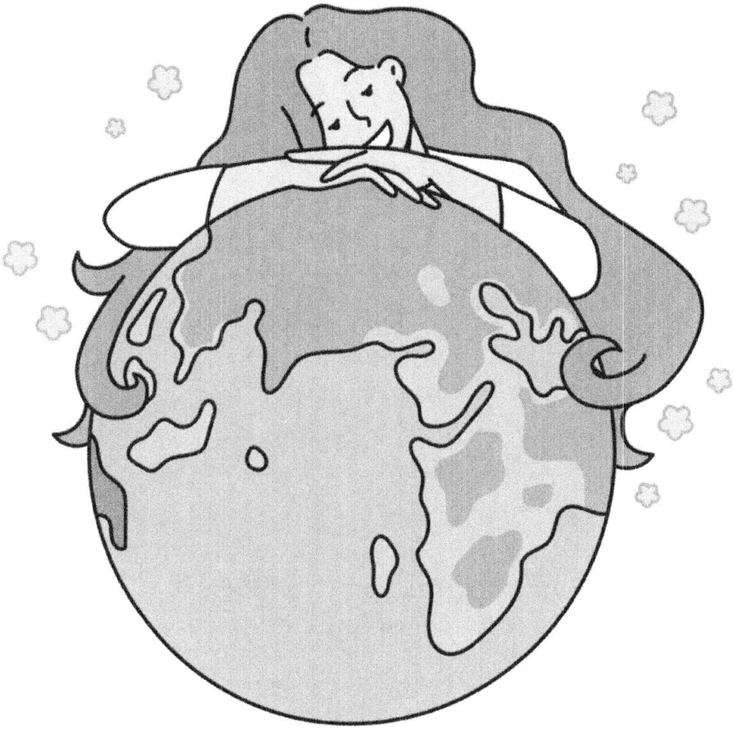

Glossary of Terms

Acupoints: Specific points on the body that correspond to different organs and systems, used in Chinese medicine, to stimulate the flow of energy and promote healing.

Acupressure: A technique that involves applying pressure to specific points on the body that correspond to different organs and systems, to stimulate the flow of energy and promote healing.

Adrenaline: A hormone that is released in response to stress, fear or excitement. It prepares the body for fight or flight by increasing heart rate, blood pressure and breathing.

Aerobic exercise: A type of physical activity that involves using oxygen to produce energy and sustain moderate to high intensity movements for a prolonged period of time, such as running, cycling, swimming or dancing.

Anger: A strong emotion that is triggered by a perceived threat, injustice or frustration and can lead to aggressive or defensive behaviour.

Antioxidants: Substances that can prevent or slow down the damage caused by free radicals, which are unstable molecules that can harm the cells and tissues of the body. Antioxidants can be found in fruits, vegetables, herbs, spices, tea, coffee, chocolate and wine.

Anxiety: A feeling of nervousness, worry or fear that is caused by uncertainty, anticipation or perceived danger and can interfere with normal functioning.

Blood pressure: The force that blood exerts on the walls of the arteries as it circulates through the body. High blood pressure can increase the risk of heart disease and stroke.

Breathing exercises: Techniques that involve controlling the rate, depth and pattern of breathing to calm the nervous system and reduce stress. Breathing exercises can also help improve blood circulation, oxygen uptake, lung function and posture.

Caffeine: A stimulant that is found in coffee, tea, chocolate, energy drinks and some medications. It can increase alertness, energy and mood by blocking the action of adenosine, a chemical that makes the brain feel sleepy. Excess caffeine can cause anxiety, insomnia and headaches.

Calling a friend: A simple way of reaching out to someone who cares about you and can offer support, comfort or advice when you are feeling low or stressed.

Calories: Units of energy that measure the amount of heat needed to raise the temperature of one gram of water by one degree Celsius. Calories are used to indicate the amount of energy that is obtained from food or expended by physical activity.

Circadian rhythms: The natural cycles of physical, mental and behavioural changes that follow a 24-hour pattern and are influenced by light and darkness.

Glossary of Terms

Carbon dioxide levels (in the body): The amount of carbon dioxide that is present in the blood and tissues of the body. Carbon dioxide is a waste product of cellular respiration and is transported to the lungs for exhalation.

Cortisol: A hormone that is released in response to stress. It helps the body cope with challenges by increasing blood sugar, suppressing the immune system and reducing inflammation. Chronic or excessive cortisol can have negative effects on health and wellbeing.

Covid pandemic: A global outbreak of the coronavirus SARS-CoV-2 that causes the respiratory disease COVID-19. It causes symptoms such as fever, cough, shortness of breath and loss of taste or smell.

Depression: A mood disorder that is characterized by persistent sadness, hopelessness, loss of interest and low self-esteem.

Distraction: A technique that involves shifting attention away from negative thoughts or unpleasant stimulus, such as pain, anxiety or boredom, onto more positive thoughts.

Dopamine: A "happiness" neurotransmitter that is involved in reward, motivation, pleasure, learning and movement.

Emotional Freedom Technique (EFT): A technique that involves tapping on specific points on the body while repeating affirmations to release negative emotions and beliefs.

Endorphins: Natural chemicals that are produced by the

brain and act as painkillers and mood boosters. Endorphins are released in response to physical activity, stress, pain or pleasure and can create a feeling of euphoria, wellbeing or relaxation.

Fluoride: A mineral that is naturally present in water, soil and some foods. It can help prevent tooth decay by strengthening the enamel of the teeth.

Gratitude: A feeling of appreciation or thankfulness for what you have or receive. It can help improve your happiness, wellbeing and relationships. Writing a gratitude journal is the practice of writing down things that you are grateful for on a regular basis, to cultivate a positive attitude and appreciate what you have in your life.

Hugging a tree: A practice of embracing a tree trunk or branch to feel connected to nature and experience its healing energy.

Journaling: A practice of writing down your thoughts, feelings and experiences on a regular basis for expression and reflection.

Jumping jacks: A type of aerobic exercise that involves jumping with the legs spread apart and the arms raised above the head, then returning to the starting position with the legs together and the arms at the sides. Jumping jacks can help increase heart rate, burn calories and tone muscles.

L-theanine: An amino acid that is found in tea leaves. It has a calming effect on the brain. It can help reduce stress, improve sleep quality and enhance cognitive performance.

Glossary of Terms

Making a plan: A process of setting goals and breaking them down into manageable steps, to increase your motivation, focus and productivity.

Meditation: A practice of focusing the mind on a single object, such as the breath, a mantra, a sound or a sensation, to achieve a state of calmness and awareness.

Metabolism: The sum of all chemical reactions that occur in the cells and tissues of the body to maintain life and produce energy. Metabolic rate is the speed at which metabolism occurs and is influenced by factors such as age, gender, body size, activity level, diet, hormones and genetics.

Mindful meditation: A type of meditation that involves paying attention to the present moment with curiosity and openness, without judging or reacting to thoughts and feelings. It can help reduce stress, improve mood and enhance awareness.

Motivation: A psychological force that drives a person to act toward a goal or desired outcome.

Overwhelmed: A state of being unable to cope with the demands or expectations of a situation, resulting in stress, anxiety or exhaustion.

Oxygen: A gas that is essential for life and cellular respiration. Oxygen is inhaled through the lungs and transported by the blood to the cells and tissues of the body. Oxygen levels can be affected by factors such as altitude, air quality, breathing rate and health conditions. The brain uses about 20% of the body's oxygen supply.

Oxytocin: A hormone that is produced by the hypothalamus and released by the pituitary gland. Oxytocin is involved in various social and emotional functions, such as bonding, trust, empathy, generosity and orgasm. Oxytocin is also known as the *love hormone* or the *cuddle hormone* because it is released when people hug, kiss or cuddle.

Psychological benefits: Positive effects on mental health and wellbeing that result from engaging in certain activities, behaviours or practices. Psychological benefits can include improved mood, self-esteem, resilience, coping skills, social skills, creativity, memory, learning and problem-solving.

Phytochemicals: A broad term referring to chemicals that are produced by plants to protect themselves from pests and diseases. They have various biological properties that can benefit human health, such as antioxidant, anti-inflammatory, anticancer, antidiabetic and antimicrobial effects.

Phytoncides: Volatile organic compounds that are a specific type of phytochemical emitted by trees. They have been shown to enhance human natural killer cell activity, reduce stress hormones, lower blood pressure and improve mood in humans who inhale them.

Polyphenols: A group of plant compounds that have antioxidant and anti-inflammatory properties. They can help protect the body from oxidative stress and chronic diseases.

Positive self-talk: A technique that involves replacing negative or critical thoughts with positive or supportive ones. Positive self-talk can help improve your mood, self-

Glossary of Terms

esteem, confidence, motivation and performance.

Power nap: A short nap of 10 to 20 minutes that can help improve alertness, mood and memory, without causing sleep inertia or affecting night-time sleep quality.

Power walk: A type of walking that involves maintaining a brisk pace and using arm movements to increase the intensity and speed of the exercise. Power walking can help burn calories, improve cardiovascular fitness and strengthen muscles and bones.

Post-Traumatic Stress Disorder (PTSD): A mental health condition that is triggered by experiencing or witnessing a traumatic event, such as war, violence, abuse, accident or disaster. PTSD can cause symptoms such as flashbacks, nightmares, intrusive thoughts, avoidance, hyperarousal, negative mood and impaired functioning.

Relaxation exercises: Techniques that help reduce physical and mental tension, such as progressive muscle relaxation, breathe exercises or guided imagery.

Rumination: A cognitive process that involves repeatedly thinking about negative or distressing events, causes, consequences or feelings, without reaching a solution or closure. Rumination can increase stress, anxiety, depression and other mental health problems.

Seasonal Affective Disorder (SAD): A type of depression that occurs during the winter months, when there is less sunlight and longer nights. It can cause symptoms such as low mood, fatigue, weight gain and social withdrawal.

TAKE A MOMENT

Self-care: The practice of taking care of your own physical, mental, emotional and spiritual needs. Self-care can involve various activities that promote health and wellbeing, such as eating well, exercising regularly, sleeping enough and relaxing often.

Self-help books: Books that offer advice or guidance on personal development, such as improving your health, happiness, relationships, skills or habits.

Self-belief: A positive attitude toward yourself that involves confidence, trust and faith in your abilities, qualities and potential. Self-belief can help you overcome challenges, achieve goals and cope with stress.

Serotonin: A *happiness* neurotransmitter that is involved in mood, sleep, appetite, memory and social behaviour.

Social media: Online platforms that allow users to create and share content, such as text, images, videos or audio and interact with other users through comments, likes, messages or groups. Social media can have various benefits and drawbacks for mental health and wellbeing, depending on how they are used.

Stress: A physical and psychological response to a perceived challenge or threat, that activates the sympathetic nervous system and the hypothalamic-pituitary-adrenal (HPA) axis and prepares the body for fight or flight. Stress can have positive or negative effects on health and performance, depending on the type, intensity and duration of the stressor.

Stress-related illness: A physical or mental condition that is caused or worsened by stress. Stress-related illnesses can include cardiovascular disease, diabetes, obesity, ulcers, irritable bowel syndrome, headaches, insomnia, depression, anxiety and substance abuse.

Tannin: A type of polyphenol that is found in tea leaves, coffee beans, red wine and some fruits and vegetables. It can have antioxidant and antimicrobial properties.

Tapping: A technique that involves tapping on specific points on the body while repeating affirmations to release negative emotions and beliefs. Tapping is also known as Emotional Freedom Technique (EFT) or Thought Field Therapy (TFT) and is based on the principles of acupuncture and energy psychology.

Therapeutic: Having a beneficial effect on health or wellbeing, especially by relieving symptoms, curing diseases or restoring function. Therapeutic can also refer to something that provides comfort, support or enjoyment.

Ticking things off a list: A method of tracking your progress and achievements by marking the tasks that you have completed on a list, to boost your confidence and satisfaction.

Trigger points (muscle knots): Small areas of tightness or contraction in the muscle fibres that can cause pain, stiffness or reduced range of motion. Trigger points can be caused by overuse, injury, stress or poor posture.

Weight reduction: The process of losing excess body fat or mass by creating a negative energy balance, that is, consuming fewer calories than expending. Weight reduction can have various benefits for health and wellbeing, such as lowering blood pressure.

Wired: A state of being alert, energised and restless, often due to caffeine, stress or lack of sleep.

Workstation: A place where you perform work-related tasks, such as a desk, a computer, a chair or a phone. A workstation should be ergonomically designed to provide comfort, support and efficiency for the user.

References

#3 – pp36-8

Effects of light on human circadian rhythms, sleep and mood.
https://www.ncbi.nlm.nih.gov/pmc/articles/PMC6751071/

Weight loss breakthrough: Sunlight is key.
https://www.medicalnewstoday.com/articles/320592

Subcutaneous white adipocytes express a light sensitive signaling pathway mediated via a melanopsin/TRPC channel axis
https://www.nature.com/articles/s41598-017-16689-4#Sec7

#9 – p51

How can audiobooks boost mental health? We're all ears!
https://www.psychologytoday.com/us/blog/worry-and-panic/201804/how-can-audio-books-boost-mental-health-were-all-ears

TAKE A MOMENT

#12 – pp56-7

A brief afternoon nap following nocturnal sleep restriction: which nap duration is most recuperative?

https://www.researchgate.net/publication/6988772_A_Brief_After noon_Nap_Following_Nocturnal_Sleep_Restriction_Which_Nap_ Duration_is_Most_Recuperative

An ultra short episode of sleep is sufficient to promote declarative memory performance.

https://www.researchgate.net/publication/5575580_An_ultra_shor t_episode_of_sleep_is_sufficient_to_promote_declarative_memory_ performance

#13 – p58

Nature and mental health: An ecosystem service perspective.

https://www.science.org/doi/10.1126/sciadv.aax0903

Irisin and FGF21 Are Cold-Induced Endocrine Activators of Brown Fat Function in Humans.

https://www.cell.com/cell-metabolism/fulltext/S1550-4131(14)00006-0

References

#17 – pp68-71

The effects of acupuncture stimulation at PC6 (Neiguan) on chronic mild stress-induced biochemical and behavioral responses.

https://pubmed.ncbi.nlm.nih.gov/19427367/

#21 – p80

The State of American Friendship: Change, Challenges, and Loss

https://www.americansurveycenter.org/research/the-state-of-american-friendship-change-challenges-and-loss/

#23 – p87

How to Identify Depression Naps.

https://www.verywellmind.com/what-are-depression-naps-5094065

#26 – p96

Your face and moves seem happier when I smile: Facial action influences the perception of emotional faces and biological motion stimuli.

https://psycnet.apa.org/record/2020-32759-001

TAKE A MOMENT

A Meta-Analysis of the Facial Feedback Literature: Effects of Facial Feedback on Emotional Experience Are Small and Variable.

https://psyarxiv.com/svjru/

#27 – p97

A study of the type and characteristics of relaxing music for college students

https://pubs.aip.org/asa/poma/article/21/1/035001/976142/

#28 – pp99-101

Owning a Pet Makes You Happier Than the Average Person, AI Analysis Reveals

https://www.psychreg.org/owning-pet-makes-you-happier/

Cat ownership and the Risk of Fatal Cardiovascular Diseases. Results from the Second National Health and Nutrition Examination Study Mortality Follow-up Study.

https://www.ncbi.nlm.nih.gov/pmc/articles/PMC3317329/

#30 – p105

Habitual tub bathing and risks of incident coronary heart disease and stroke

https://heart.bmj.com/content/106/10/732

Resources and Further Reading

The following links to resources and further reading is intended to give you some ideas of where to go for further information and advice. Inclusion in this list does not imply endorsement of any of the organisations, websites or apps. Please use your own judgment as to the accuracy and usefulness of the information, products or services they offer.

~~~~~~~~~~

There are some really great websites that cover many aspects of mental health and wellbeing.

Mind

https://www.mind.org.uk/

Mental Health Foundation

https://www.mentalhealth.org.uk/

NHS

https://www.nhs.uk/mental-health/

Mental Health UK

https://mentalhealth-uk.org/

HelpGuide

https://www.helpguide.org/

Young Minds

https://www.youngminds.org.uk/

Age UK

https://www.ageuk.org.uk/information-advice/health-wellbeing/

~~~~~~~~~~~

There are also many specialist websites and charities that can help with specific concerns.

Anxiety UK

https://www.anxietyuk.org.uk/

Depression UK

https://www.depressionuk.org/

Loneliness

https://www.webofloneliness.com/

PTSD UK

https://www.ptsduk.org/

Stress Management Society

https://www.stress.org.uk/

The Sleep Charity

https://thesleepcharity.org.uk/

Resources and Further Reading

If you are looking for more information about some of the techniques discussed in this book, these links may help.

British Acupressure Council

https://acupuncture.org.uk/

British Association for Music Therapy

https://www.bamt.org/

British Association of Mindfulness-Based Approaches (BAMBA)

https://bamba.org.uk/

British School of Meditation

https://www.teaching-meditation.co.uk/

Emotional Freedom Technique (EFT)

https://eftinternational.org/

Gratitude Initiative

https://gratitudeinitiative.org.uk/

The Forest Bathing Institute

https://tfb.institute/

Mindfulness Association

https://www.mindfulnessassociation.net/

Pets as Therapy

https://petsastherapy.org/

TAKE A MOMENT

The following are useful apps that offer help at those times when you need to take a moment for yourself. Some of these apps require a paid membership to use them, some have a free trial option and some are free.

They can be downloaded from the Apple Store or from Google Play.

Breethe

Calm

Catch It

Chill Panda

Happify

Headspace

Living Life to the Full

Mindshift CBT

Muse

My Possible Self

Talkspace

Thrive

Worry Tree

One Last Thing...

Thank you for reading this book.

If you feel that it has helped you, I would really appreciate it if you could spare the time to leave a review on Amazon.

What did you like about this book?

How did it help you?

Did I miss anything that you would have liked to have seen included or done differently?

Would you recommend it to others?

If you have any tips or techniques that have really helped you and that you would like to share, please drop me a line at the email address below. 😊

Feel free to get in touch at:

jo@inanutshellbooks.com

Fast Fix Finder

This is a fast index to help you to find the Fast Fix you need in a hurry. The numbers in the right-hand column refer to the *Fast Fix* numbers.

Anxiety	17, 28, 32
Calm	7, 10, 16, 19, 25
CALM Technique	24
Depression	23, 32
Escape	9, 13, 24
Gratitude	11
Low Self-Esteem	22, 32
Kick-Start	1, 2
Loneliness	29
Low Mood	4, 27, 32
Motivation	2, 8, 31
Overwhelm	6, 30
Reassurance	28, 33
Refresh/Refocus	6, 12, 14, 15, 18, 20, 30
Relax	19, 22, 24, 25
Sleep	22, 23, 24
STARS Exercise	20
Stress	5, 16, 17, 19, 25
Superpower Lift	22

Index

30-day challenge
  progress, 122, 141
  tracker, 122
acupoints, 68, 116
acupressure, 68, 75
affirmations, 43, 135, 141
afternoon, 47, 49, 61, 64, 144
anger, 45, 46, 99, 105, 112
antioxidants, 53, 138, 141
anxiety, 26, 37, 40, 51, 55, 58, 68, 69, 75, 77, 88, 93, 94, 95, 100, 105, 108, 109, 134, 135, 137, 139, 141
audiobook, 49, 50, 65
bacteria, 40, 105
balance, 48, 58, 76, 77, 78, 79, 102, 106, 141
bath, 103, 105, 119, 146
birthday, 112
blood pressure, 36, 40, 58, 70, 99, 105, 133, 134, 142
body temperature, 56, 104, 105
brain, 35, 37, 95, 96, 97, 105, 110, 134, 136, 137
breathing exercises, 20, 23, 40, 44, 70, 79, 86, 93, 94, 98, 120, 133, 134, 135, 137, 139

caffeine, 53, 134, 142
calm down, 61, 70, 93
CALM technique, 91
calories, 58, 136, 139, 142
carbon dioxide, 40, 58, 135
Christmas, 40, 106
circadian rhythms, 36, 143
comfort, 44, 49, 55, 86, 89, 94, 99, 101, 102, 134, 141, 142
concentration, 56, 58, 77, 97
Covid pandemic, 72, 135
creativity, 58, 138
depression, 26, 33, 37, 50, 51, 58, 68, 70, 75, 87, 88, 100, 105, 139, 141, 145
diary, 54, 80, 81, 82
disappointment, 112
distraction, 47, 50, 65, 86
emotional freedom technique (EFT), 24, 75, 76, 77, 118, 135, 141, 149
endorphins, 67, 68, 97
energy, 23, 31, 33, 41, 47, 58, 61, 64, 66, 67, 68, 75, 77, 87, 109, 122, 133, 134, 136, 137, 141
equilibrium, 111, 112

escape, 49, 51, 65, 89, 90, 116
essential oils, 40
  frankincense, 40
  lavender, 40
evening, 38, 80, 82, 106
exercise, 39, 41, 42, 47, 67, 68, 69, 78, 79, 85, 90, 94, 95, 99, 109, 117, 118, 119, 120, 133, 134, 136, 139, 140
exercise, aerobic, 67, 136
exhaustion, 68, 137
family, 19, 27, 55, 61, 75, 89, 102, 103, 106, 130
fed up, 55
fluoride, 53
focus, 20, 42, 47, 52, 56, 58, 61, 64, 77, 106, 122, 137
friends, 20, 24, 27, 33, 48, 49, 51, 55, 75, 80, 81, 82, 101, 102, 103, 106, 112, 119, 121, 129, 130, 134
goals, 107, 137, 140
gratitude, 54, 136
gratitude journal, 54, 136
health, 19, 21, 35, 43, 47, 67, 105, 109, 116, 135, 137, 138, 139, 140, 141, 142, 143, 144, 147, 148
hope, loss of, 111
hormones
  adrenaline, 33, 47, 65, 66, 67
  cortisol, 40, 47, 52, 66, 67, 135
  oxytocin, 40, 100, 104
hugging, 39, 40, 99, 102, 138
journal, 54, 80, 81, 82, 136
Kindle, 49
laughter, 96
lifespan, 101
lifestyle, 102, 109
loneliness, 93, 102, 105
low mood, 23, 31, 87, 88, 139
L-theanine, 52, 136
lunchtime, 41, 117
meditation, 43, 44, 116, 137, 149
meridian points, 68, 75, 77
metabolism, 67, 137, 144
mood, 20, 23, 26, 31, 36, 54, 56, 58, 78, 79, 87, 88, 97, 98, 99, 102, 106, 112, 122, 134, 135, 136, 137, 138, 139, 140, 143
morning, 31, 32, 35, 36, 37, 38, 41, 100, 103, 116
motivation, 23, 31, 33, 46, 47, 88, 99, 106, 135, 137, 139
muscle tension, 58, 139, 141
muscles, 35, 62, 71, 86, 95, 96, 97, 105, 136, 139
music therapy, 65, 97, 98, 99, 117, 146
nature, 38, 40, 58, 59, 79, 89, 109, 111, 112, 136, 143
neck, 62, 71, 72, 79, 117

Index

negative, 47, 50, 51, 104, 108, 109, 135, 138, 139, 140, 141
negative ions, 104
neurotransmitters
  dopamine, 31, 96, 100
  serotonin, 31, 37, 96, 100, 105
optimistic, 62, 104
overwhelm, 43, 47, 93
oxygen, 35, 40, 58, 79, 97, 133, 134, 137
pet therapy, 99, 100, 101, 146
phytochemicals, 53
phytoncides, 40
plan, make a, 106, 108, 137
polyphenols, 53
positive self-talk, 109, 138
post-traumatic stress disorder (PTSD), 68, 75, 139, 148
posture, 63, 72, 78, 79, 134, 141
power nap, 56
power walk, 65, 67
productivity, 58, 137
psychological benefits, 75, 97, 137, 140
reassurance, 40, 99, 102
reflection, 85, 136
refocus, 43, 94, 129
refresh, 51, 57, 64
relaxation, 40, 48, 51, 52, 53, 70, 75, 85, 86, 87, 89, 90, 91, 94, 95, 98, 99, 100, 101, 104, 105, 118, 121, 136, 139
rest, 32, 40, 75, 85, 87, 88, 112, 142
sadness, 87, 88, 112, 135
sanctuary, place of, 87, 89, 91, 116, 120
seasonal affective disorder (SAD), 38, 139
self-belief, 83
self-care, 105, 115, 124
self-esteem, 135, 138, 139
self-esteem, low, 135
self-indulgent, 21, 129
shoulders, 62, 71, 72
shower, 103, 104, 105, 119
sleep, 36, 38, 51, 56, 57, 58, 85, 86, 87, 88, 89, 91, 101, 104, 118, 136, 139, 140, 142, 143, 144
sleep, lack of, 88, 142
smile, 91, 95, 96, 97, 123, 145
social connections, 102
social media, 80
STARS exercise, 78, 118
stress, 23, 40, 41, 42, 49, 52, 55, 58, 65, 66, 67, 68, 69, 70, 75, 77, 90, 93, 94, 95, 97, 99, 100, 101, 104, 106, 109, 133, 134, 135, 136, 137, 138, 139, 140, 141, 142, 145, 148
stretching, 36, 62, 63, 64, 119
summer holiday, 106

Superpower Lift, 69
support group, 88
tannins, 53
tapping, 75, 76, 77, 135, 141
tea, 33, 52, 53, 116, 133, 134, 136, 141
therapeutic, 50, 67, 68, 81, 93
therapist, 26, 88
tired, 23, 56, 64, 71, 78, 88, 103, 112
tree, hugging a, 40

trigger points, 72
wake up, 35, 36, 57, 85, 86, 103
walking, 33, 37, 50, 64, 65, 67, 120, 130, 139
weight, 67, 77, 139
wellbeing, 21, 58, 67, 87, 102, 104, 105, 116, 124, 135, 136, 138, 140, 141, 142, 147, 148
wired, 66, 99
workstation, 72, 142

In A Nutshell Books.com

Printed in Great Britain
by Amazon